THE HELPING TRADITION IN THE BLACK FAMILY AND COMMUNITY

THE HELPING TRADITION IN THE BLACK FAMILY AND COMMUNITY

Gift

JOANNE M. MARTIN & ELMER P. MARTIN

NATIONAL ASSOCIATION OF SOCIAL WORKERS
SILVER SPRING, MD

Designed by Steffie Kaplan

Library of Congress Cataloging in Publication Data

Martin, Joanne Mitchell.
    The helping tradition in the Black family and community.

    Bibliography
    1. Afro-American families. 2. Self-help techniques—History. 3. Afro-Americans—Social conditions.
I. Martin, Elmer P. II. Title.
E185.86.M375 1985   305.8'96073   85-10511
ISBN 0-87101-129-8

Printed in U.S.A.

To Bertina Martin, Lisa Martin, Jamin Elmer Keene, and all the children of our family members and friends, in the hope that they will carry on the helping tradition.

ACKNOWLEDGMENTS

For their encouragement and assistance in the preparation of our study and for carrying on the helping tradition themselves or for passing it on to us, we would like to acknowledge the following persons: Alberta Cason; the late Harriet Martin; the late Bessie Mitchell; Essie Mae Russell; Jeremiah Mitchell, Sr.; Jeremiah Mitchell, Jr.; Lillian McCray; Ed McCray; Ella Mae McCrimon; Theodore McCrimon; the late Lillian Lewis; the late Bruce Lewis, Jr.; Elsie and Wilbert Minnis and family; Arlena Cason; George Cason; the late Emanuel Cason, Sr.; the late Emanuel Cason, Jr.; Peter Cason and family; Sylvester Cason and family; Hilda Gilyard; Maggie Wingard; Edna Jackson and Nikki Jackson; Tulani Salahu-din; Elizabeth Byrd; Elizabeth Peavy; Sam Waweru; Ronald Rooks and family; Deborah Pierce; the late Mary Pierce; Cottrell Wesson; Darryl Talley; Thom Thompson; the late Jerome Ward; "Pop" Hampton and family; Lee Roy Carter; Rev. Lewis Keene; Franes Keene; Elma "Mickey" Goodman and family; Mary Sanders and family; Nancy Martin and family; Marcella Howard and family; Gaynell Martin and family; Emogene Martin and family; Adebelle Martin and family; Florence Martin and family; James Martin; Elroy Martin and family; Delbert Martin and family; Albert Martin; Charles Martin; Maurice Martin; Mary Elsie Lewis and family; Gary Lewis and family; Arthur Lewis; Leroy Lewis and family; Jackie Lee and family; Leonard Lewis; Perry Lewis; Richard Lewis; Luther Lewis; Stan Lewis; Tony Lewis; Merita Lewis; Milton and Chris Morris and Chipper; Stephanie and Annie Morris and family; Martha Waterman; Laura Nicholson; Gloria Greer; J. Van Melton; and Louisa Goodman.

CONTENTS

INTRODUCTION

According to Hobhouse—the late noted British sociologist—*tradition* is "the link between past and future; it is that in which the effects of the past are consolidated and on the basis of which subsequent modifications are built."[1] Hobhouse maintained that

> the tradition of the elders...furnishes the prescribed rule of dealing with the ordinary occasions of life....It furnishes the appropriate institution for providing for each class of social needs, for meeting common dangers, for satisfying social wants, for regulating social relations. ...What is handed on is not merely a set of ideas, but the whole social environment; not merely certain ways of thinking or of acting, but the conditions which prescribe to individuals the necessity for thinking or acting in certain specific ways if they are to achieve their own desires.[2]

This definition of *tradition* is classic. But, according to noted social scientists, black Americans have no history, no culture, and no traditions. Even some sociologists who have produced major studies on black people maintain that blacks have no traditions. For example, Odum, after devoting much of his scholarly work to the study of blacks, claimed that they have "no pride of ancestry."[3] Myrdal, who produced a highly regarded study on black people, categorically stated that if blacks have a tradition, it is warped or pathological.[4] Kardiner and Ovesey, after an extensive probe into the black psyche, concluded that blacks have "no intrapsychic defenses—no pride, no group solidarity, no tradition."[5] Silberman, in a sensitive portrayal of the plight of black people, wrote that blacks "lack the common history and cultural traditions which the other groups share."[6] Glazer and Moynihan, agreeing with the views of a great many others, gave practically every ethnic group in this country a strong tradition, but, in referring to black people, noted that "the Negro is only an American and nothing else. He has no values and culture to guard and protect."[7] Even Frazier, the renowned black sociologist, stated that "when one undertakes the study of the

1

Negro, he discovers a great poverty of traditions."[8] He went on to say:

> ...because of the absence of stability in family life, there is a lack of traditions [and hence] life among a large portion of the urban Negro population is casual, precarious, and fragmentary. It lacks continuity and its roots do not go deeper than the contingencies of daily living.[9]

The views expressed in this book run counter to those of Frazier and others. In examining the black helping tradition, we propose that this tradition developed from the black extended family's struggles against patriarchy and its emphasis on mutual aid and cooperation among members of different social classes or status groups. We further propose that, from its origin in the extended family, the black helping tradition spread into practically every phase of black community life. As Gutman put it: "Kin obligations among Afro-Americans survived enslavement, and enlarged social obligation emerged out of kin obligation."[10] Scholars, however, challenge even the black helping tradition. For example, Handlin, the Pulitzer Prize-winning historian and authority on ethnicity and immigrant life, said that urban blacks lack the "tradition of philanthropy" and "communal solidarity" that white immigrants brought with them to America.[11] He wrote:

> In the character of their communal life, the Negroes...are farthest removed from the experiences of earlier immigrant groups....They have not developed the integrated pattern of voluntary organizations that gave their predecessors understanding of the problems of metropolitan life and aid in dealing with them. It was significant, for instance, that the array of hospitals, orphanages, homes for the aged, and other philanthropic institutions established and supported by the nineteenth century immigrants had no counterpart among the Negroes. As a result, they could not find the help they needed within the context of the group; and the group lacked this means of giving its identity significant expression.[12]

Our investigation presents conclusive evidence that nineteenth-century blacks, in particular, had a powerful sense of mutual aid and communal solidarity that grew out of a strong black family tradition. As early as 1909, Du Bois provided ample documentation of the existence throughout black American history of black extended families, orphanages, old folks' homes, benevolent societies, fraternal orders, protest and uplift organizations, hospitals, churches, women's clubs, and so forth.[13] With other scholars joining Du Bois to furnish additional evidence that blacks do indeed have a tradition, it is amazing that writers such as Handlin could make such a claim. Yet, it is not the aim of this book to prove that black people have traditions. Commonsense judgment suggests that it is not possible for a people to have been in this country for over 400 years, to have been forced to separate themselves from the dominant national life, to have had to face daily the deadly terror of oppression, and still not to have created values and practices that they deemed not only necessary for their survival and advancement but worthy of being handed down from generation to generation. As Ellison, the black novelist, said: "Men have made a way of life in caves and upon cliffs, why cannot Negroes have made a life upon the horns of the white man's dilemma?"[14]

When one undertakes a serious and unbiased study of the life of black Americans, he or she will find that blacks have many traditions—of protest, of religion, of music, of family life, and so on. But, as we already noted, this book focuses on the helping tradition simply because this tradition cuts across a broad spectrum of black life and culture. Consequently, the investigation of this tradition produces a deep understanding of black life in this country. For, in the context of Hobhouse's definition of *tradition,* the black helping tradition is not merely the handing down of a set of ideas; rather, it is the handing down of the "whole social environment" and a prescription of how blacks should deal with the "ordinary occasions of life." It is not the practice of unrelated, fragmented, and aimless beliefs, but a phenomenon that is significantly intertwined with the whole culture of black people and the quest of blacks for survival and advancement. Even as this tradition declines—and it most assuredly is in a state of sharp and rapid decline—a study of it highlights how it has changed and where it is heading.

Although, as we noted, others have examined the black helping tradition, their works largely have been descriptive studies that attempted to counter racist notions that blacks are an irresponsible, dependent people.[15] For example, in her study of the contributions of black people to social services, Lindsay sought to challenge the belief that "Negroes throughout their history in America have been recipients of philanthropic and benevolent endeavors to an extent quite disproportionate to their percentage in the population.[16] Her work is a descriptive essay of black people's participation in self-help endeavors during certain periods in American history.

Later studies on the black helping tradition have been, for the most part, responses to the demand by major social work bodies for the inclusion of more ethnic-oriented material in social work curricula. For instance, Pollard's study on black people's self-help efforts developed from his experience of having gone through an undergraduate and master's program in social work without having learned much about the historical roots of black people's participation in American social welfare.[17] So, as valuable as his study and others like it are, they are still primarily descriptive.

This book strives to do more than describe or document the existence of the black helping tradition. It offers a theory regarding its origin, development, and decline. In this sense, the book is more analytic than descriptive. In other words, it does not merely strive to prove that the black helping tradition exists, but it examines the social, psychological, and historical forces from which the tradition grew.

A *theory* generally is a broad set of related propositions or concepts designed to explain a social phenomenon. A fundamental assumption of the research on which this book is based is that a pattern of black self-help activities developed from the black extended family—particularly the extended family's major elements of mutual aid, social-class cooperation, male-female equality, and prosocial behavior in children. Furthermore, we propose that this pattern of black self-help was spread from the black extended family to institutions in the wider black community through fictive kinship and racial and religious consciousness.

The following are key concepts that recur throughout:

■ *Black helping tradition* refers to the largely independent struggle of blacks for their survival and advancement from generation to generation.

■ *Black extended family* consists of a multigenerational, interdependent kinship system held together basically by a sense of obligation to the welfare of members of the kin network.

■ *Mutual aid,* a dominant element in extended family life, involves a reciprocal effort of family members to pool the resources necessary for survival and growth.

■ *Social-class (status-group) cooperation* is the endeavor of family members of different income, educational, and social-class levels to downplay class distinctions in giving and receiving aid.

■ *Male-female equality* is the adherence of black men and women to certain conventions that promote the welfare of the family through an emphasis on sexual equality and a deemphasis on matriarchy and patriarchy.

■ *Prosocial behavior* involves the attitudes and practices of cooperation, sharing, and caring that black adults consciously strive to instill in black children so the tradition of black self-help will be passed on to future generations.

■ *Fictive kinship* is the caregiving and mutual-aid relationship among nonrelated blacks that exists because of their common ancestry, history, and social plight.

■ *Racial consciousness* is the keen awareness by many black people of their history and condition as a people and their overwhelming desire to uplift their race to a state of dignity and pride.

■ *Religious consciousness* (in the context of this book) refers to deliberate attempts by blacks to live according to those religious beliefs that call for acts of charity and brotherliness and neighborliness toward one another as a means of coming closer to God and of carrying out God's will.

The delineation of these key concepts helps to explain the major forces that are responsible for the birth and growth of the black helping tradition, but it does not explain the forces that have worked against this tradition. The following are four major elements that have impeded the development of the black helping tradition:

■ *Racism* occurs when one people deliberately and systematically subjugates another people that it holds to be inferior. Racism has had a dual, adverse impact on the life and helping tradition of black people. On the one hand, it has caused blacks to be so oppressed that they have had to develop self-help strategies for sheer survival. On the other hand, it has fostered the ideology that blacks are a childlike, dependent people incapable of doing for themselves without the guidance of white people. This ideology has been used by racists as a justification for keeping black people from gaining the first-class citizenship necessary for full self-determination.

■ The *bourgeoisie ideology* is largely a middle-class suburban-based stance that places heavy emphasis on individualism, social-status seeking, and the acquisition of material goods through such legitimate means as hard work, education, and civic responsibility.

■ The *street ideology* is largely a lower-class urban-based stance that places heavy emphasis on individualism and the acquisition of material goods through such deviant or illegitimate means as manipulation, conning, or criminal activity.

■ *Patriarchy*—the notion of a male-centered or male-dominated family and society—strikes particularly hard at the black helping tradition. Therefore, it is dealt with at length throughout this book. In essence, the study challenged the prevailing social science myth that the key to the stability of the black family and the black community is a strong patriarchy. This myth is so deeply rooted in the social sciences and in social work that it has been accepted largely as an unquestionable fact. Advancers of this myth generally start out by portraying the black family as matriarchal and end up by presenting patriarchy as a way toward stability, health, and virtue.

Moynihan's controversial study of the black family is a clear example of the patriarchal myth. Moynihan put together a statistical hodgepodge which allegedly provided empirical evidence that the black family is characterized by a "tangle of pathologies which is at the heart of the deterioration of Negro society."[18] He wrote:

> In essence, the Negro community has been forced into a matriarchal structure which, because it is so out of line with the rest of American society, seriously retards the progress of the group as a whole, and imposes a crushing burden on the Negro male and, in consequence, on a great many Negro women as well.[19]

This book attempts to show that few of the many adverse forces facing black people have done more than patriarchy to destroy the black helping tradition. Yet many social scientists and social workers continue to view patriarchy as a cure for the ills of the black family and black community. As Millet explained:

> Contemporary white sociology often operates under a . . . patriarchal bias when its rhetoric inclines toward the assertion that . . . racial inequity is capable of solution by a restoration of masculine authority. Whatever the facts of the matter may be, it can also be suggested that an analysis of this kind presupposes patriarchal values without questioning them, and tends to obscure both the true character of and the responsibility for racist injustices toward Black humanity of both sexes.[20]

The theory of the origin, development, and decline of the black helping tradition has been stated, and the key concepts have been defined. But, before we conclude this introduction, it is appropriate to raise a relevant question: Of what value is this study?

A study of the black helping tradition has a social value. It may help those who have been conditioned to think that blacks have no traditions to gain more appreciation and respect for black life and culture. And as far as black people are concerned, it may give them a greater conviction of their worth as a people. As Herskovits wrote, "A people that denies its past cannot escape being a prey to doubt of its value today and of its potentialities for the future."[21]

Herskovits's view, however, runs counter to those of scholars with an assimilationist orientation. One such great scholar is Cox, who maintained that "Negroes cannot revert to a cultural history and mythology of such a character as would inspire a significant in-group sentiment of nativistic pride."[22] Another black sociologist, Patterson, argued vociferously that blacks must "spurn tradition" and "abandon their search for a past, must indeed recognize that they lack all claims to a distinctive cultural heritage."[23] Such scholars tend to think of tradition as a dead weight that holds black people in antiquity while all about them a modern world is steadily changing and developing and leaving them behind. These thinkers believe that the ways of the elders are old-fashioned, irrelevant guidelines for the present and future lives of the new generation, and they associate the past with the nightmarish episodes of slavery, lynching, and Jim Crowism—events and conditions blacks would rather forget. But, given the subjugated status of blacks in American society, the racist efforts to make blacks feel inferior, and the low self-esteem and self-hatred that is so pervasive among and immobilizing and debilitating to blacks, practically any study that seriously analyzes the prosocial behavior and care-giving efforts of black people has the potential of being a source of black pride and, therefore, of carrying on the work of such black scholars as W. E. B. Du Bois, Carter G. Woodson, and many others who devoted their lives to a rediscovery of black traditions in the belief that pride and identity are necessary for a healthy and well-adjusted black personality.

A study of the black helping tradition also has an academic or educational value. Almost every major study that has documented black self-help and care-giving endeavors has been motivated by a desire to fill gaps in the literature, particularly the social work literature. For example, Ross, in her study of the black heritage in social welfare, wrote that "this textbook was devised and developed as a corrective for omissions and deficiencies in the existing literature on social welfare, and especially by the absence of any extensive body of materials illustrative of the black heritage and experience in this area of knowledge."[24]

Social workers have acknowledged the need for content of this nature in the social work curricula. It is indeed peculiar to find that although most histories of social work go back to the English Poor Law, they skip over the helping tradition of blacks during slavery, the Underground Railroad movement, the abolitionist movement, and even the Freedmen's Bureau, which was the first massive governmental effort at caregiving. This book strives to make up for some of the deficiencies in the literature. Its aim is to introduce social work students and practitioners to the contributions that black people have made to social welfare and to what blacks have done and are capable of doing to help themselves.

However, the book offers more than just a documentation that blacks have created orphanages, old-folks' homes, and the like. More significantly, it presents a guiding theory—a systematic way of viewing the black family and the black community. This theory not only explains the forces responsible for the rise, development, and decline of the black helping tradition, but it suggests a model for social work practice from a black perspective. It teaches social workers and others what black people have deemed important for their survival and advancement. For example, in looking for the sources of strength and indicators of stability and health in the black family, social workers may examine the extent to which elements of mutual aid, social-class cooperation, male-female equality, and prosocial behavior in children are present. Furthermore, racial and religious consciousness and a prosocial attitude may be more indicative of a healthy black personality than anything suggested by Sigmund Freud; it may be more important for social workers to view the black community from the standpoint of its efforts and ability to uplift itself than to be preoccupied with deviance, deficits, and pathologies.

And, of course, the study should be of value to social scientists, educators, and lay persons who are interested in the life and culture of black people in this country. In the end, the value of a study of this nature is its ability to offer new information and insights. If this book has done little more than that, it will have made a small but significant contribution to this neglected area.

REFERENCES

1. Leonard T. Hobhouse, *Social Evolution and Political Theory* (New York: Columbia University Press, 1911), p. 34.

2. Ibid., pp. 34–35.

3. Howard Odum, *Social and Mental Traits of the Negro* (New York: AMS Press, 1910), p. 39.

4. Gunnar Myrdal, *An American Dilemma* (New York: Harper & Bros., 1944), p. 928.

5. Abram Kardiner and Lionel Ovesey, *The Mark of Oppression* (New York: W. W. Norton & Co., 1951), p. 384.

6. Charles Silberman, *Crisis in Black and White* (New York: Random House, 1964), p. 166.

7. Nathan Glazer and Daniel P. Moynihan, *Beyond the Melting Pot* (Cambridge, Mass.: M.I.T. Press, 1963), p. 53.

8. E. Franklin Frazier, "Traditions and Patterns of Negro Family Life in the United States," in E. B. Reuter, ed., *Race and Culture Contacts* (New York: McGraw-Hill Book Co., 1934), p. 194.

9. Ibid.

10. Herbert G. Gutman, *The Black Family in Slavery and Freedom, 1750–1925* (New York: Pantheon Books, 1976), p. 229.

11. Oscar Handlin, *The Newcomers* (Cambridge, Mass.: Harvard University Press, 1959), p. 105.

12. Ibid.

13. See W. E. B. Du Bois, *Efforts for Social Betterment Among Negro Americans* (Atlanta, Ga.: Atlanta University Press, 1909).

14. Ralph Ellison, *Shadow and Act* (New York: Random House, 1964), pp. 315–316.

15. See Du Bois, *Efforts for Social Betterment Among Negro Americans;* Inabel B. Lindsay, "The Participation of Negroes in the Establishment of Welfare Services, 1865–1900," unpublished doctoral dissertation, University of Pittsburgh School of Social Work, 1952; and Edyth Ross, *The Black Heritage in Social Welfare, 1860–1930* (Metuchen, N.J.: Scarecrow Press, 1978).

16. Lindsay, "The Participation of Negroes in the Establishment of Welfare Services."

17. William L. Pollard, *A Study in Black Self-Help* (San Francisco: R & E Associates, 1978), p. 1.

18. Daniel Patrick Moynihan, *The Negro Family: A Case for National Action* (Washington, D. C.: U.S. Department of Labor, Office of Policy, Planning & Research, March 1965), p. 75.

19. Ibid.

20. Kate Millet, *Sexual Politics* (Garden City, N.Y.: Doubleday & Co., 1970), p. 54.

21. Melville J. Herskovits, *The Myth of the Negro Past* (Boston: Beacon Hill Press, 1958), p. 32.

22. Oliver C. Cox, *Caste, Class, and Race* (New York: Doubleday & Co., 1948), p. 567–568.

23. Orlando Patterson, "Toward a Future that Has No Past—Reflections on the Fate of Blacks in the Americas," *Public Interest,* 27 (Spring 1972), p. 61.

24. Ross, *The Black Heritage in Social Welfare,* p. viii.

1 THE HELPING TRADITION IN TRADITIONAL AFRICA AND IN SLAVERY

Blacks had a solid reputation for being polite, hospitable, and charitable long before they were brought to this country in slave ships. Park, one of the earliest European explorers of Africa, expecting to find Africans in a state of savagery and chaos, was startled by the high level of organization and civility among African people.[1] He found that Africans from the most highly complex nation to the simplest tribal unit were not lacking in art, religion, trade, law, government, architecture, education, and other tangible and intangible products associated with a people fashioning their own culture and society. Park was particularly fascinated by and grateful for the warm hospitality extended to him by Africans during his travels. Describing Africans as a "people of manners and dispositions so gentle and benevolent," he wrote:

> It is impossible for me to forget the disinterested charity, and tender solicitude, with which many of these poor heathens, from the sovereign of Sego, to the poor women who received me at different times in their cottages, when I was perishing of hunger, sympathized with me in my suffering, relieved my distresses, and contributed to my safety.
> ...It is surely reasonable to suppose, that the soft and amiable sympathy of nature, which was spontaneously manifested toward me in my distress, is displayed by these poor people, as occasion requires, much more strongly toward persons of their own nations and neighbourhood, and especially when the objects of their compassion are endeared to them by the ties of consanguinity.[2]

The charitable impulse was indeed deeply rooted in tradi-

11

tional African life and culture. As Blyden, the nineteenth-century Africanist described it, "We, and not I is the law of African life."[3] Mbiti held that the cardinal point of African philosophy could be summarized in the saying: "I am, because we are; and since we are, therefore I am," which means that traditional Africans did not see themselves as individuals with a concern for self over the group, but saw the group as a corporate part of the individual personality.[4] Modern African leaders are trying to revive the spirit of that traditional African law and philosophy. They see the extended family as the foundation for mutual responsibility and call for "the extension of the African family spirit to the nation [and from] the nation, or even the continent to embrace the whole society of mankind."[5]

AFRICAN EXTENDED FAMILY

Despite the diversity of traditional African societies, one feature shared by nearly all of them was that life was organized around the family. Kinship bonds were so strong in traditional Africa that sometimes smaller family units (nuclear families) would become part of a larger extended family network, and the larger extended family network would often make up a clan, and several clans would make up the entire tribe or community. The traditional African kinship system was "like a vast network stretching in every direction, to embrace everybody in any given local group," linking each person to everyone else.[6]

It was the extended family ties that were the basis for caregiving. The helping tradition among African people was, as Park surmised, stronger when "the objects of their compassion" were "endeared to them by the ties of consanguinity." Nyerere, a modern African leader, statesman, and scholar, commented that the members of the traditional African family "lived together and worked together; and the result of their joint labour was the property of the family as a whole."[7] He continued:

> The results of their joint effort were divided unequally between them, but according to well-understood customs. And the division was always on the basis of the fact that every member of the family had to have enough to eat, some simple covering, and a place to sleep, before any of them (even the head of the family) had anything extra. The family members thought of themselves as one, and all their language and behavior emphasized their unity. The basic goods of life were "our food," "our land," "our cattle."...Each member of the family recognized the place and rights of the other members, and although the rights varied according

to sex, age, and even ability and character, there was a minimum below which no one could exist without disgrace to the whole family.[8]

That "no one could go hungry while others hoarded food, and no one could be denied shelter if others had space to spare" meant that "the individuals or the families within a tribe were 'rich' or 'poor' according to whether the whole tribe was rich or poor," and it meant that so long as "the tribe prospered, all the members of the tribe shared in its prosperity."[9]

Patriarchy

Patriarchy was at the core of traditional African family life. Men generally were the unquestioned heads of the family, as well as the leaders, authority figures, and decision makers in the African community. Men, particularly older men, had dominant roles as chiefs, priests, healers, rainmakers, prophets, teachers, sages, warriors, counselors, and power wielders. Men resolved disputes, handed down laws, meted out punishment, handled land transactions, performed civil and religious rituals and ceremonies, and otherwise determined practically all the affairs of family and community life.

The polygamous nature of African family life basically served the interests of men. It brought them as many wives as they could afford. It gave them status and prestige in the community, provided them with enough children to ensure the continuance of the family lineage and a sufficient number of workers to tend the animals and crops, and extended their kinship ties, which increased their influence, wealth, authority, and power throughout the community.

Although patriarchy was an essential feature of African life, the traditional African family and community did not allow it to thwart or frustrate their mutual-aid thrust. No matter how much wealth or power a man attained, he could not place his individual interests above those of the group. A man could not form a social class with other men of his rank and look down on or exploit the rest of the African community. Even the chiefs, priests, and other high authority figures could not hoard while others were unsheltered or hungry. Even as a patriarch, a man had to raise his children to concern themselves with the well-being of the community, and it was difficult for him to mistreat his wives without being called to account by both their kin and his kin and perhaps by the whole African community. He was required by African law and society to ensure their basic survival needs and their dignity as women, wives, and mothers.

Role of Women

In the traditional African family and community, women generally played subordinate roles. They were expected, even required, to obey the authority of their husbands and to show them a high degree of respect and deference. They were expected to do their share of menial agricultural labor and practically all the household chores. And they were expected to receive their status and prestige largely from the status and prestige accorded to their husbands by the community. Although each wife in a polygamous situation had her own compound or household and although women in their roles as traders in the marketplace often received a portion of what they sold and hence gained some degree of social and economic independence, overall, they were subordinate to men. Therefore, regardless of their importance to the community and their limited independence, they were still bound by the decisions of men.

Prosocialization of the Children

In no role were women considered as important to African family and community life as in the bearing of children. As Mbiti noted, the failure to bear children brought women a shame and disgrace that they could hardly erase, regardless of how sympathetic their husbands and others might be to their plight.[10] Traditional Africans emphasized both the living and the dead. Therefore, having children ensured not only the continuity of the family lineage but the immortality of the family members.

Children were brought up to take on the prosocial ways of their elders. Kenyatta, speaking of the education of the children of the Kikuyu tribe of Kenya, held that "the bigger things" children learn are the habits of helping their parents and working under the system of reciprocity with other people.[11] Early in life, they learn how important collective endeavors are in building the community. "House-building, cultivation, harvesting, digging trap-pits, putting up fences around cultivated fields, and building bridges," as well as marital ceremonies, making war, and engaging in religious and recreational activities are done by the group.[12] Kenyatta wrote:

> Children learn this habit of communal work like others, not by verbal exhortations so much as by joining with older people in such social services. They see the household and friends building a house for somebody, when everybody brings poles for the upright or grass for thatching. They go with their relatives to help in another man's garden, building his house or his cattlepens or grainary. They help in provision

of his marriage feasts or brewing beer for a kinship ceremonial party. All help given in this way is voluntary, and kinsfolk are proud to help one another. There is no payment or expectation of payment!....The whole thing rests on the principle of reciprocal obligations.[13]

The mutual-aid tradition of the extended family guaranteed that children could not be raised to put their egos or interests above those of the group. Children might engage in sibling rivalry, compete for the favor of their fathers, or be competitive in games and rituals with other children, but they were educated, taken through various rites, and reared to view the fellow members of their community as their brothers and sisters and to consider the welfare of the group to be as sacred as their individual welfare. This kind of socialization assured that the helping customs of traditional Africa would be passed down through the generations.

Fictive Kinship

It is easy to see, then, that one did not have to be a relative by blood or marriage to receive help in traditional African society. Everybody in the community was treated like kin. Kenyatta said that so deep was the feeling of helping and sharing that even those who did not reciprocate sentiments of neighborliness could expect to receive help, especially in times of emergency.[14] Selfish people and individualists were frowned on, and the heroes and heroines of the African community were generally people who were willing to check selfish impulses for the welfare of the group.

Early Africans, known for their judicial institutions and respect for legal authority, generally made the helping tradition a part of the laws of the society.[15] In many instances, a person was brought before the public court not just for offenses such as thievery but for being selfish and unneighborly, and especially for treating productive assets as if they were his or her private property and using them in ways not consonant with the general welfare of the people.

RETENTION OF THE AFRICAN HELPING TRADITION

To what extent was the helping heritage of traditional Africa carried over into black life in this country? This question is at the heart of a long-standing scholarly debate between Frazier and Herskovits.[16] Frazier maintained that "probably never before in history has a people been so completely stripped of its social heritage as the Negroes who were brought to America.[17] Herskovits countered that it is "the force of African tradition" that has made "for the special cultural traits that mark off the Negro" in this country.[18] He held that the helping tradition is such a "deep-seated drive in Negro life [that] it is difficult if not impossible to account for it satisfactorily except in terms of 'the traditional African past.'"[19]

Several powerful forces militated against the retention of the African tradition among blacks brought to this country as slaves. First, as Quarles stated, "the ancestor of the American Negro came from no single region [was] of no single tribe or physical type, had no common tongue," and had no single type of political institution; thus, it was hardly likely that an entire family or community would be kept together or that the customs of a particular group of blacks would express the culture of a particular tribe.[20] Second, the all-powerful slave master was adamantly opposed to blacks holding on to their African heritage. Third, many American slaves soon gave up trying to maintain their African tradition and culture. Rather, they concentrated on finding new ways to survive in their new hostile environment, which created the likelihood that many blacks who were born in this country would know little about their African heritage or place little importance on knowing about it.

But there also were forces that allowed for the retention of Africanisms by American blacks. Regardless of the region, tribe, or community, the helping tradition was deeply rooted in the African way of life. It was to be found almost everywhere that African people existed. It was not possible for Africans in this country to recreate the totality of their cultures; however, they could more easily retain the noninstitutional than the institutional aspects of their cultures in the New World. The helping tradition was so much a part of the hearts and habits of African men and women that even when severed from its original institutional anchors, it could not help but remain strong in the new land.

Although the slave master forbade Africans to display outward forms of their culture, the slavery system demanded cooperation between the slaves, especially because most work demanded it. Furthermore, if slaves had not cooperated with one another, it is not likely that they could have survived the oppressive rigors of the system. Slavery inadvertently reinforced the African helping tradition. Slaves had to build their own homes, which they constructed according to African architecture and from what they had learned from white men. Both the skills of housebuilding and the practice of Africans working communally to build homes for their people were carried over into slavery. The hunting, trapping, and gardening that slaves had to do to supplement the scanty rations they received from the slave master were additional skills that blacks had learned in Africa. Moreover, since slaves were generally responsible for taking care of their sick, they relied heavily on their traditional African use of herbs, spices, ointments, and linaments to cure a host of ailments. In a sense, the slave doctor was a prototype of the African medicine man, and the conjurer on the slave plantation, who was responsible largely for the psychic and spiritual health of the slaves, resembled the "witch doctor" in many traditional African communities. And, what is most important is that the slaves learned a vital lesson from their African ancestors: to take the resources their environment and nature had to offer and make a way for themselves.

The helping tradition in slavery was further reinforced by the emergence of leaders on the plantation. It is not true that only ignorant laborers of so-called common stock were brought to this country. African community leaders of all persuasions were forced onto slave ships, and many of them clandestinely sought to keep alive the African spirit. As Herskovits wrote, "The worker of magic, the wise old woman, the man whose personality made him a leader in cooperative effort or in successful revolt thus retained a hold on the people."[21]

Furthermore, Africans newly arrived on American soil were constantly being brought to the plantations, which kept alive their African heritage in the memory of the blacks already there. This memory is indicated in the following account by an ex-slave in 1837:

> I was born in Africa, several hundred miles up the Gambia River. Fine country dat; but we are called heathen in dis Christian—no, I don't know what to call it—in dis enlightened heathen country. But the villagers in that country are kind. When you go into house, first question is, have you had anything to eat? Bring water, you wash, and den eat much you want; and all you got do is thank them for it—not one fip you pay. If you are sick, nurse you, and make you well—not one fip you pay. If you want clothing, one woman put in two knots warp, one put in two knots filling, and so on; den men weave it, and you cut just such garment you like—not one fip you pay.[22]

It appears, then, that the helping tradition developed by black people in this country is a carryover from the traditional African past. As Magdol concluded, "Among slaves and freedmen, an ethos of mutuality was the expression of traditional African consciousness and morality."[23] This tradition took on different forms as blacks responded to the exigencies of their situation, and it was no longer rooted in the rituals and institutions of their indigenous culture. Nevertheless, the tradition was strong among blacks in this country and emerged as a dominant force in all areas of their lives.

HELPING TRADITION AND THE SLAVE FAMILY

Slavery destroyed the traditional African family by uprooting it from its aboriginal heritage, but it did not destroy the strong feeling for family that the slaves had deep within their souls. If anything, it enhanced this feeling. To take people from their families and homeland and bring them motherless to a strange land is to make those people long even more for their families or to be a part of a family in the New World. To understand, as the slaves did, that at any moment a spouse, a sister, a brother, a mother, or a father could be sold and never be seen or heard of again made family ties even more precious. This strong sense of family explains why some slaves who had escaped to semifreedom worked for years to buy relatives or risked their lives going back into the jaws of slavery itself to rescue their kin. It also explains why some slaves who could have escaped did not. It was often less painful to them to be slaves with their kin and loved ones than to be free without them.

The extended family was the basis of the black helping tradition among the slaves. As Gutman held, "Adaptive kin obligations were transformed by the slaves themselves into larger social and communal obligations."[24] Four crucial elements of family life among the slaves were key to the development of caregiving in the slave community: (1) the breakdown of patriarchy and the concomitant rise of black male-female equality and cooperation, (2) the mutual-aid network, (3) the prosocialization of children, and (4) status-group cooperation.

Breakdown of Patriarchy

Slavery stripped black men of the patriarchal authority they had in Africa. The slave master was the chief patriarch—the father, the authority figure, and the decision maker. The wife and children of the black man had to obey the slave master above all. If the male slave told his wife to do one thing and the slave master demanded that she do the contrary, naturally she had to obey the master. The African man in slavery was reduced to less than the subservient level of his woman. Indeed, his status was reduced to the level of his children, for if he ordered his children to do something and the master ordered them to do something else, the children had to obey the slave master. The male slave could not help but feel an overwhelming sense of powerlessness.

Everywhere and every day on the plantation, the male slave experienced serious assaults on his manhood, the most serious being "his inability to protect his wife from the sexual advances of white men and the physical abuse of his master."[25] Because a man who could not protect his woman from being raped and abused by another was not a man in traditional African society, many male slaves preferred to marry women from other plantations. "They did not want to marry a woman from their own plantation and watch as she was beaten, insulted, overworked, or starved without being able to protect her.[26] They would rather suffer the pain of separation than experience such an extreme sense of helplessness.

Black Male-Female Equality and Cooperation

As cruel and as dehumanizing as slavery was, it gave a crude type of equality to the black man and the black woman. It was a "de facto equality," according to Hodge, "the equality of cattle in a herd"—the equality of being subjected to the same toil, torture, and brutality.[27] In Genovese's view, it was an equality that was "much greater" than that between men and women of the white family.[28] And Blassingame held that this equality "led to the creation of America's first democratic family. . .where men and women shared authority and responsibility."[29] It was for this reason, as Davis noted, that slaves "transformed that negative equality which emanated from the equal oppression they suffered as slaves into a positive oppression of equality: the egalitarianism characterizing their social relations."[30]

Slavery equalized the black man and black woman in the most important world on the plantation: the world of work. There was no work that the black man did that the black woman did not do as well. Du Bois suggested that if feminists need proof that women are the occupational equals of men, all they need do is look at the black woman in slavery. "That she could and did replace the white man as laborer, artisan, and servant," he pointed out, "showed the possibility of the white woman doing the same thing. . . . Moreover, the usual sentimental arguments against women at work were not brought forward in the case of Negro womanhood."[31] Truth put the equality of the black woman in the world of work in more illustrative terms:

> I have plowed, and planted, and gathered into barns, and no man could head me—and ain't I a woman? I could work as much and eat as much as a man (when I could get it), and bear de lash as well—and ain't I a woman.[32]

The equalization of the sexes came about partly from the conscious effort by slave masters to defeminize black women. The slave masters did so not only by working black women as hard as black men and subjecting them equally to punishment and brutality, but by forcing black women, in many instances, to wear men's clothing and treating them in a manner so crude and coarse as to leave them fully aware that they were not placed on a pedestal. As Truth said: "Nobody ever helped me into carriages, or ober mud puddles, or gives me any best place. . . . And when I cried out with a mother's grief, none but Jesus heard."[33]

Matriarchy

Although the black patriarchy was undermined in slavery and a negative equality was forced on black men and women, a matriarchy did not develop, contrary to popular thought in the social sciences. Several factors worked against the development of a matriarchy. First, not only did women do the same type of work as did men on the plantation, but they had to perform "certain duties considered women's work," such as cooking, cleaning, sewing, and washing clothes.[34] This type of work brought them lower, not higher, status. According to Owens, the slave master sometimes punished male slaves by forcing them to do so-called women's work, and "so great was their shame before their fellows," he wrote, "that many [men] ran off and suffered the lash on their backs rather than submit to this discipline."[35]

A second factor that stifled the development of a matriarchy was the black woman's role as a breeder of children and a sex object. Many black women were bred like animals to ensure the master a steady supply of workers. In addition, black women often were pregnant because they were treated as sex objects who had to satisfy the desires of both black men and white men. It was the sexual relations which black women had with white men that social scientists claim gave them the power that black men did not have. Bernard held that "because they were useful in the role of breeders as well as that of workers, female slaves were strategically better off than males."[36] Frazier went so far as to claim that the intimate relations between slave women and white men caused a positive transfer of the white culture to the blacks.[37]

However, instead of gaining power, the black woman had more babies in addition to undergoing the helplessness and psychological pain of frequently being raped. And, unlike the black woman in traditional Africa, who gained great esteem and status from having children, the black woman in slavery generally suffered from impaired health, increased suffering and grief, and a shortened life. Kemble, the white wife of a slave owner, recorded this account in her diary:

> In considering the whole condition of the people on this plantation, it appears to me that the principal hardships fall to the lot of the women. . . .Fanny has had six children; all dead but one. She came to beg to have her work in the field lightened. Nanny has had three children; two of them dead. . . .Leah has had six children; three are dead. Sophy. . .is suffering fearfully; she had had ten children born; five of them are dead. Sally had had two miscarriages and three children born, one of whom is dead. She came complaining of incessant pain and weakness in her back. Sarah. . .had had four miscarriages, had brought seven children into the world, five of whom are dead, and was again with child. She complained of dreadful pains in the back, an internal tumor which swells with the exertion of working in the fields; probably, I think, she is ruptured. . . .Molly['s]. . .was the best account I have yet received; she had had nine children, and six of them were still alive. . . .There was hardly one of these women. . .who might not have been a candidate for a bed in a hospital, and they had come to see me after working all day in the fields.[38]

Even the black "mammy," who is "presumed to capture the essence of the Black woman's role in slavery" was no more than a powerless beast of burden like any other slave, despite her alleged propensity to be "sassy" to whites.[39] In slavery, most black women were field workers—not domestic servants or mammies. And even the mammies were not exempt from hard work. Besides raising the master's children, they had a number of difficult chores, in addition to the care of their own families. Furthermore, their role as mammies did not exempt them from cruelty. Indeed, their proximity to the master and his family guaranteed that they suffered daily from the frustrations, rage, and anger of the white members of the household. One ex-slave recalled seeing his mother, a slave mammy, being attacked by both the master and the master's daughter:

> He came down, called my mother out, and, with a hickory rod, he beat her 15 or 20 strokes, then called his daughter and told her to take her satisfaction on her, and she did beat her until she was satisfied. Oh! it was dreadful, to see this girl whom my poor mother had taken care of from her childhood, thus beating her, and I must stand there, and did not dare to crook my fingers in her defense.[40]

The roles black women played in slavery, according to Martin and Martin, made them "special captives" of oppression—not the wielders of power, influence, and status associated with a matriarchy.[41]

MUTUAL AID

The equalization of black men and black women and the cruel circumstance of slavery made it necessary for black slave men and women to cooperate for survival, and this cooperation was essential in establishing the black helping tradition. What is even more significant is that the slave family, like the traditional African family, consisted of more than just a husband, a wife, and their dependent children; hence, mutual aid among relatives also was essential for survival. As Owens stated: "The slave family was a unit with extensions."[42] It included relatives by "marriage," by blood, and by adoption. Slaves took in parentless children and made sure that new slaves were absorbed into slave families and initiated into slave life. As in traditional Africa, individuals in slavery rarely sought to go it alone. The isolated and stultifying world of the plantation placed slaves in a common predicament—one in which their survival depended on the communal spirit of extended family ties. "The extended slave family," Owens held, "frequently arose to augment or replace the regular family split up by slavery's misfortunes. There were deaths resulting from disease, accidents, and natural causes that left wives husbandless and children without parents. Then there were the family breakups caused by the slave trade."[43]

Role of Fictive Kinship

The slave family included both kin and nonkin. Gutman wrote that

> fictive, or quasi, kin played yet other roles in developing slave communities, binding unrelated adults to one another and thereby infusing enlarged

slave communities with conceptions of obligations that had flowed initially from kin obligations rooted in blood and marriage. The obligations to a brother or a niece were transformed into the obligations toward a fellow slave or a fellow slave's child, and behavior first determined by familial and kin obligation became an enlarged social obligation.[44]

These enlarged social obligations were expressed in a number of ways: by helping new slaves to adjust to plantation life, by raising crops in common to supplement the paltry rations issued irregularly by the slave masters, by tending the sick, by giving comfort to those slaves broken in mind and spirit, by burying the dead, by having recreation together, by worshipping together, by sharing scarce resources, by planning revolts and escapes, and by enforcing a code of conduct to create more unity because the behavior of one slave could jeopardize the welfare of all. Two areas that demonstrate the spirit of mutual aid and provide evidence of fictive kinship were the care of older slaves and the rearing of children.

Care of the elderly. The aged, like women, were "special captives" in that they were subjugated to special oppressive treatment. The old slaves could no longer work as hard as they could when they were younger, and this lowered their worth in the eyes of the slave master. Many times, young slaves would help the old slaves to do their work or meet their quotas, but their help did not stop many of the old slaves from getting in the way and "moderately disrupting operations by their slow labor and need for rest."[45] Owens held that masters often assigned old slaves the lighter duties or classified them as "half hands," and cut their rations. And occasionally when old slaves were unable to work because of illness, blindness, or just old age, they were "set aside in the woods to fend for themselves."[46] Frequently, the master would free the old slaves to rid himself of the responsibility of caring for them or he would sell the old slaves cheaply to anyone who would buy them.[47]

The strong sense of kinship made the life of the old slaves easier to bear. As in traditional Africa, the aged were looked up to and respected in the slave community. They were given an honorable place in the family and were often viewed as the heads of the slave families. They were given the important roles of raising the children and instilling in them the values that were essential for survival. Even adult slaves had much to learn from the old slaves. As Genovese said, "the slaves, including the children, looked to the needs of their old people and treated them with a respect and deference that offset humiliations heaped on them by condescending, not to mention, unkind whites."[48]

In Traditional Africa and Slavery 23

Care of children. Although work in the fields left slave parents little time to look after their children, children nevertheless became a primary concern of the slave community. If a parent became sick, the children never feared that they would be without food and shelter. The same was true if a parent died. And should a parent suffer the worst fate that could befall a slave, to be sold away from his or her relatives or loved ones, the children never needed to fear that they would be motherless or fatherless—left alone to fend for themselves in a cruel and hostile world. For they would be absorbed naturally into existing households and raised by relatives or nonkin.

A difficult task of the old slaves and slave parents was to teach slave children how to be good slaves. According to Blassingame and other historians, slave children often had a great deal of freedom to roam the plantation; many became the playmates of white children virtually on a basis of equality and were hardly aware that they were slaves.[49] However, when young people reached the age when they were expected to do serious work on the plantation, slave parents suddenly had to make them realize that they were only a piece of property.

Parents had to go through a process of "breaking" their children, that is, beating out or driving out all the rebellious, aggressive, insubordinate, and hostile behaviors that might get the children (or the parents, or both) into serious trouble with the slave master. As Genovese stated, the slave parents "had to teach their children how to survive in an extraordinarily dangerous world."[50] Any mistake a child made, such as looking the master in the eye, failing to lower his or her head when addressing the master, or not addressing the master with the appropriate "yes, sir" or "no, sir," could mean more severe punishment from the master than the slave parents were likely to give. As adults, the slaves had to clearly understand that any breach of the etiquette of slavery could mean punishment as severe as death. Therefore, slave children had to be broken early to know their place and to be taught that they were not the equals of white children, even those they played with and viewed as friends. To whites, all the slaves were "niggers" and that is what the whites called them.

Not all the socialization of the children was geared toward making them good slaves. A part of rearing children was to teach them the prosocial values necessary for the survival of the slave family and community. Usually while the parents were in the fields, older slaves took primary responsibility for rearing the children. The older slaves taught the older children to care for the younger ones, both kin and nonkin. They passed down a black heritage of caring, helping, and sharing. The older slaves instilled in the young slaves prosocial values of mutual cooperation and support, teaching them to feel a sense of obligation for the welfare of black people, while trying to shield them from the rawest brutalities of slavery.

Parents demanded strict obedience from children, not only to prepare them for dealing with the slave master, but to protect the other slaves from a vengeful slave master who might mete out punishment to the group for the wrongdoing of an individual. "Children should be seen and not heard," for example, was a maxim that warned children not only to keep from orally confronting or challenging the master, but to keep silent about the affairs of the family and the slave community because the slave master frequently interrogated the children about the behavior and attitudes of their parents and other adults.

However, as in traditional Africa, children were taught prosocial values not only by precept but by example. They saw how slaves came together to assist a new slave on the plantation, rallied to care for the aged and the infirm, shared their scanty resources, and treated even nonkin like blood relatives. And they knew how proud adults were when children exhibited similar behavior.

Status-Group Cooperation

Slavery did not permit social classes to emerge among the slaves. But it did allow for the emergence of status groups. The three broadest status groups on the plantation were the house slaves, the field slaves, and the skilled slaves. These groups cooperated with each other for mutual survival.

Although "popular lore sometimes labeled house servants 'Uncle Toms,' pawns of the slaveholders and betrayers of their slave brothers, house slaves and field slaves were generally closer than popularly perceived."[51] The extended family had a great deal to do with this closeness. Many house slaves had family members who were field slaves and found it difficult to look down on their mothers, fathers, brothers, sisters, and other relatives and friends who were field slaves. Also, it was not unusual for house servants to marry field slaves to do "double duty as field hands," particularly during the harvest season, and, in many cases, to live in the quarters with field slaves.[52]

That many house slaves envied the lives of field slaves

made it difficult for many house slaves to view themselves as being in a higher status or a superior position. House slaves often received better food, clothing, and shelter, but their lives were not such as to arouse envy or jealousy in field slaves. They had to work just as hard as the field slaves, while being "at the beck and call of the master day or night" and subject to his "every capricious, vengeful, or sadistic whim."[53] At the end of a grueling workday, the field slave enjoyed a modicum of freedom. He could take off the mask of obsequiousness he had to wear before white people. He could laugh and play and love and tend his garden and even tell stories and jokes about the master. He could pray, rest, and share moments with his wife and children and even show his anger. But, as Litwack noted:

> [A house slave] had to learn to be a "good nigger," to submit to indignities without protest, to submerge his feelings, to repress his emotions, to play "dumb" when the occasion demanded it, to respond with the proper gestures and words to every command, to learn the uses of flattery and humility, to never appear overly intelligent.[54]

The house servants' strong sense of solidarity with field slaves resulted in the former being of invaluable service to the latter. Being better off economically than field slaves often meant that the house slaves were in a better position to distribute to the field slaves the master's food, clothing, household utensils, liquor, tobacco, and other needed and desired items. House slaves were particularly helpful in passing on information that field slaves needed to plan escapes and to survive the daily onslaughts of their existence. In this regard, Owens said that "planters discovered all too recurringly that talk about the sale of slaves, runaways, and resistance was communicated to bondsmen in question by domestics."[55]

The skilled blacks also cooperated with field slaves, for they often had relatives among them. Genovese held that although skilled blacks enjoyed high status and "a reputation for being the proudest and most independent of all slaves," no evidence exists that they had "widespread contempt for the field hands."[56] The skilled blacks often brought their trades with them from Africa; thus, they immediately became valuable to the slave master because they could not only use their crafts on the plantation but could be hired out as well, bringing the master an additional income. Skilled blacks often taught younger blacks their trade and many times secretly taught slaves how to read and write. Their travels from plantation to plantation and from town to town often brought them in close contact with other slaves and free blacks, making them valuable sources of news, gossip, and vital information. Most of all, their abilities provided living proof to field slaves that black people were just as capable of learning and mastery as white people and, more important, that blacks were capable of making a living independently of the paternalistic slave master. Although slavery allowed little room for upward mobility, the image of the skilled black—learned, proud, and independent—gave slaves a higher status to aspire and an awareness that the crafts and trades taught them by the skilled black would be invaluable not so much in slavery as when they would all be free.

RELIGIOUS AND RACIAL CONSCIOUSNESS

Religious consciousness and the budding racial consciousness among the slaves reinforced the mutual-aid effort that stemmed from the extended family and fictive kinship. Worshipping God served as a source of therapy for slaves even though the slave masters distorted Christianity to advance the interests of slavery. The slave masters took the brotherhood and sisterhood out of Christianity and made it a religion of obedience to, and worship of, the slave master. The most important teaching of the Holy Bible, then, was this:

> Slaves, obey your human masters with fear and trembling; and do it with a sincere heart, as though you were serving Christ. Do this not only because you want to gain their approval; but with all your heart do what God wants, as slaves of Christ. Do your work as slaves cheerfully as though you served the Lord, and not merely men. Remember that the Lord will reward everyone, whether slave or free, for the good he does.[57]

Following the dictates of this biblical injunction, the preachers were instructed to give slaves such catechisms as these:

Question: Who gave you a master?

Answer: God gave him to me.

Question: Who says you must obey him?

Answer: God says that I must.

Question: What did God make you for?

Answer: To make crop.

Even though they were forced to listen to religious instruction designed to make them content with slavery, the slaves worshipped God in their own way when they stole away at night and worshipped in their own "invisible" churches. The worship of God became an important aspect of the psychological and spiritual survival of the slaves. It gave them a sense of personal significance and worth in a world in which they were defined not as human beings but as property. The belief that God recognized them as equals to whites, that God recognized each of them personally as one of his children, and, more important, that God was on their side served as powerful medicine for sick souls and frustrated hopes. The belief that although the slave master might be more powerful than the slave, he was not more powerful than their God gave slaves a feeling of psychological and spiritual advantage over the slave master.

The "institutional" black church was to become a dominant care-giving institution, second in importance only to the black extended family. But even the "invisible" church of the slave was a case of mutual aid in action in that slaves came together as one big family, seeking a greater resource than themselves in the physical, psychological, and spiritual battle for survival. The Christian religious ideology of caring, giving, and loving reinforced in the slaves that sharing meant not only striving for their survival but acting the way God intended human beings to act.

Racial consciousness among the slaves was nowhere more evident than in protest and rebellion. Any protest or rebellion, whether individual or collective in nature, required the cooperation and support of nearly all the slaves and an awareness that blacks were suffering a common oppression. Here, again, the extended family was important because many quests for freedom began when slaves could no longer stand to see their relatives and loved ones being brutally treated and abused. This strong identification with the suffering of one's relatives, whether extended or fictive kin, was the basis for a budding racial consciousness among the slaves.

It was not easy for slaves to protest or rebel against their plight. The master took extreme care to stamp out any signs of rebelliousness by his property. Toward this end, he used torture, propaganda, religion, and murder. Nevertheless, consciously aware of their common oppression; urged on by rebellious, race-conscious leaders; and unable to bear witness to the abuse of their kin, loved ones, and fellow slaves, rebellious slaves used both subtle and overt means to rebel against their plight. By doing so, these slaves risked being punished, maimed, or killed. Of course, most slaves did not rebel; even though the African helping tradition was strongly evident in the slave community, there were always individual slaves who deviated from the norm. There were always slaves who helped the slave master to oppress other slaves, and there were always slaves who were selfish, evil, and hostile toward other slaves. But, just as in traditional Africa, the selfish person or individualist was a danger to the overall survival of the slave community. Therefore, the heroes and heroines—those given the most respect—were those who expressed just as much concern for the well-being and freedom of other slaves as they did for themselves.

REFERENCES

1. See Mungo Park, *Travels in Africa* (New York: M. McFarlane, 1901).
2. Ibid., pp. 352 and 296–297.
3. Edward Wilmot Blyden, *African Life and Customs* (London, England: C. M. Phillips, 1908), p. 30.
4. John S. Mbiti, *African Religion and Philosophy* (Garden City, N.Y.: Doubleday & Co., 1970), p. 14.
5. Julius Nyerere, *Freedom and Unity* (London, England: Oxford University Press, 1966), p. 170.
6. Mbiti, *African Religion and Philosophy,* p. 136.
7. Julius Nyerere, *Freedom and Socialism* (New York: Oxford University Press, 1968), p. 170.
8. Ibid., p. 336.
9. Ibid.; and Nyerere, *Freedom and Unity,* p. 168.
10. Mbiti, *African Religion and Philosophy,* p. 144.
11. Jomo Kenyatta, *Facing Mt. Kenya* (New York: Vintage Books, 1965), p. 109.
12. Ibid., p. 113.
13. Ibid., pp. 113–114.
14. Ibid., p. 114.
15. For a discussion of the African judicial and legal systems, see Richard W. Hull, *Munyakare African Civilization Before the Batuuree* (New York: John Wiley & Sons, 1972), chap. 4, pp. 101–129.
16. See chap. 1, "Forgotten Memories," in E. Franklin Frazier, *The Negro Family in the United States* (Chicago: University of Chicago Press, 1969), pp. 2–17; and Melville J. Herskovits, *Myth of the Negro Past* (Boston: Beacon Hill Press, 1958).
17. Frazier, *The Negro Family,* p. 15.
18. Herskovits, *Myth of the Negro Past,* pp. 298–299.
19. Ibid., p. 164.

20. Benjamin Quarles, *The Negro in the Making of America* (New York: Collier Books, 1964), p. 16.

21. Herskovits, *Myth of the Negro Past,* p. 141.

22. John W. Blassingame, *Slave Testimony* (Baton Rouge: Louisiana State University Press, 1977), p. 124.

23. Edward Magdol, *A Right to the Land: Essays on the Freedmen's Community* (Westport, Conn.: Greenwood Press, 1977), p. 11.

24. Herbert G. Gutman, *The Black Family in Slavery and Freedom 1750–1925* (New York: Pantheon Books, 1976), p. 229.

25. John W. Blassingame, *The Slave Community* (New York: Oxford University Press, 1972), p. 172.

26. Ibid.

27. Merle Hodge, "The Shadow of the Whip: A Comment on Male-Female Relations in the Caribbean," in Orde Coombs, ed., *Is Massa Day Dead?* (Garden City, N.Y.: Doubleday & Co., 1971), p. 114.

28. Eugene D. Genovese, *Roll, Jordon, Roll* (New York: Pantheon Books, 1974), p. 501.

29. Blassingame, *The Slave Community,* p. 178.

30. Angela Davis, *Women, Race, and Class* (New York: Random House, 1981), p. 18.

31. W. E. B. Du Bois, *Gift of Black Folk: The Negroes in the Making of America* (1924; Reprint, New York: AMS Press, 1972), p. 262.

32. Bert James Loewenberg and Ruth Bogin, *Black Women in Nineteenth-Century Life* (University Park: Pennsylvania State University Press, 1976), p. 235.

33. Ibid.

34. Leslie Howard Owens, *This Species of Property* (New York: Oxford University Press, 1976), p. 195.

35. Ibid.

36. Jessie Bernard, *Marriage and Family Among Negroes* (Englewood Cliffs, N.J.: Prentice-Hall, 1966), p. 68.

37. Frazier, *The Negro Family in the United States,* p. 169.

38. J. A. Scott, ed., *Frances Ann Kemble's Journal of a Residence on a Georgia Plantation in 1838–1839* (New York: Alfred A. Knopf, 1961), pp. 224–241.

39. Davis, *Women, Race, and Class,* p. 18.

40. Blassingame, *Slave Testimony,* pp. 132–133.

41. See Elmer P. Martin and Joanne M. Martin, "The Black Woman: Cultural and Economic Captive," in Pauline Kolenda, ed., *Contemporary Cultures For and Against Women* (Houston, Tex.: University of Houston Press, 1981), p. 235.

42. Owens, *This Species of Property,* p. 210.

43. Ibid.

44. Gutman, *The Black Family,* p. 220.

45. Owens, *This Species of Property,* p. 47.

46. Ibid.

47. Ibid., p. 49.

48. Genovese, *Roll, Jordon, Roll,* p. 523.
49. Blassingame, *The Slave Community,* pp. 94–96.
50. Genovese, *Roll, Jordon, Roll,* p. 510.
51. Owens, *This Species of Property,* p. 106.
52. Genovese, *Roll, Jordon, Roll,* p. 339.
53. Blassingame, *The Slave Community,* pp. 157–158.
54. Leon F. Litwack, *Been in the Storm So Long* (New York: Alfred A. Knopf, 1979), p. 158.
55. Owens, *This Species of Property,* p. 115.
56. Genovese, *Roll, Jordon, Roll,* pp. 392–393.
57. *The Holy Bible, Good News Bible: The Bible in Today's English Version* (New York: American Bible Society, 1976) Eph. 6:5–9.

In Traditional Africa and Slavery

2 THE HELPING TRADITION AMONG FREE BLACKS

Whether they had been set free or had run away, had been born in a nonslave state or free on foreign soil, had bought their own freedom or been bought by other blacks, there were large populations of free or nonslave blacks in the nonslave and slave states, North and South. Freedom, though, was not without cost. Forced into a cruel, segregated life, the free black had no right to vote, could not testify in the courts against a white man, had no right to bear arms, was forced to observe a curfew, and had to do work classified as "nigger work" or to receive lower wages than whites when doing comparable skilled work. For the most part poor, propertyless, and degraded, the free black had to find shelter in slums, shanties, cellars, back alleys, or in the open air and was required to carry with him everywhere legal documents declaring his freedom lest he be declared a runaway, jailed, hired out, or sold—be made a slave.[1]

Life was rough and brutal for the free black; yet, it was better to be free than to be a slave. The slave was under the total authority of the white slave master. He could be bought and sold like cattle, "transferred for life a thousand miles or more," and his "family, wife, and children could be legally and absolutely taken from him."[2] He could own nothing, make no contracts, hold no property, could not hire out his labor, could not legally marry, could not control his children, could neither question the master's authority over the family nor control the master's lust for slave women. He had no right of petition, no right of education and religion, no hope, as long as he was a slave, of realizing his fullest human promise and potential or of becoming a full-fledged American citizen.[3] Free black life was degraded, but slavery was the ultimate degradation.

STATUS-GROUP COOPERATION AMONG BLACKS AND SLAVES

The slaves and the free blacks lived in two different worlds, but these two worlds were inextricably connected. The free blacks did not forget their brothers and sisters in slavery. For example, colonization societies wanted to send free blacks back to Africa or to other foreign soils, but one reason for the blacks' rejection of this plan was that to agree to such a scheme would mean having to abandon the slaves, "their brethren by the ties of consanguinity, suffering, and wrong."[4]

The free blacks' sense of identification with slaves was especially strong when they had relatives who were slaves. As Berlin said: "If racial ideology effectively united whites and separated them from most blacks, it also sealed the bonds of racial unity between the mass of free Negroes and slaves."[5] Slaves and free blacks often came together in churches, in the streets, in homes, and in secret places known only to them. They helped feed, clothe, shelter, and hide one another when necessary and passed on information vital to each other's survival. In a sense, they were like spies in a foreign territory, for many of their meetings, plots, and schemes had to be clandestine. And they were well aware that whites looked on the relationship between slaves and free blacks with the utmost suspicion. The racial consciousness among them was strong because they faced a common oppression and a common enemy and had a common desire to be free.

The ties between free blacks and slaves often made the difference between bondage and freedom because the black helping tradition was strongest in the efforts of free blacks to gain freedom for the slaves. Despite the extreme efforts slave masters took to stamp out any signs of rebellion by their property and to keep others from rescuing or freeing their slaves, both slaves and free blacks took a defiant stance toward bondage.

As stated previously, the slaves took great risks to rebel against their plight. They formed Maroon communities in mountains and swamps, engaged in acts of sabotage, feigned illness and stupidity to avoid heavy work, planned open revolts and rebellions, and even resisted "through desperate acts of self-violence," such as chopping off fingers and toes, eating dirt so they would be unfit for work, and committing suicide or putting to death their newly born children so those children would not suffer the cruelties of slavery.[6]

If slaves were to be both alive and free from slavery, they usually had to depend on the assistance of free blacks as well as that of many sympathetic whites. Free blacks, many of them who had tasted the bitterness of slavery, generally felt it was their duty and responsibility to help other blacks obtain their freedom. Some free blacks saved money for years, undergoing many hardships and sacrifices to free a single slave; often, when they had raised the money for the purchase of a slave, the slave master would raise the price, forcing them to work even longer. Many free blacks felt so obligated to free the slaves that some went so far as to lend their manumission papers to runaway relatives and friends, taking the serious risk of losing their own freedom by trusting that the runaways would escape and return the papers. This feeling of duty was even greater when free blacks had friends and relatives in slavery who they wanted to be free. Blacks who fled from slavery could not have succeeded without the help of kin and friends (and a number of white people). It was no wonder then that "so often did runaways take refuge with friends and relatives that masters usually looked first to them when searching for their missing property."[7]

One area of freedom fighting in which free blacks working with white people were most active was the Underground Railroad. Some blacks, such as William Still, allowed their home to serve as one of the "stations" in which slaves found shelter, food, comfort, rest, and encouragement. But others risked their lives going back into slavery to lead relatives, friends, and strangers to freedom. The most heroic example of an ex-slave rescuing slaves was Harriet Tubman, who went back into slavery 19 times, rescuing over 300 slaves.[8] Even Josiah Henson, known as the "real Uncle Tom," led 200 slaves to freedom.[9] Some free blacks and some whites even abducted slaves. And when the slaves were in the free states, it was the free blacks who saw to it that they were hidden, fed, clothed, sheltered, and protected from the all-pervasive slave catchers seeking to return them to bondage.

Free blacks were equally active in the abolitionist movement and its effort to abolish slavery. Frederick Douglass, Sojourner Truth, Francis Ellen Watkins, David Walker, and Martin Delaney were just a few of the many blacks whose lives were a living testament not only to the black helping tradition but to the great black heritage of protest.

FROM KIN CONSCIOUSNESS TO RACIAL CONSCIOUSNESS

Gutman maintained that fictive kinship was the primary device for "enlarging social relationships among slaves."[10] This was true in the self-contained world of the slaves, where it was indeed easy for slaves to see one another as belonging to one big family. But, in the larger world of the free blacks, it was more than kin consciousness that made for blacks helping other blacks. Kin consciousness became racial consciousness when blacks became increasingly aware of their common predicament and came to believe that their survival and advancement were enhanced more by coming together as a race than by their individual efforts.

The feeling of oneness that evolved from their ties to their extended family and to their fictive kin found a higher expression in racial consciousness. Racial consciousness meant considering other blacks as your brothers and sisters—all fighting a common battle to be free. It also meant having pride in the accomplishments and contributions of black people and confidence in their ability to overcome obstacles and to advance.

Free blacks were among the first generation of race-conscious blacks to call themselves "race men" and "race women"— men and women whose primary concern was the survival, uplift, and liberation of black people.[11] These race men and race women expressed their consciousness in numerous ways. They defended the race when it came under attack by racist propaganda designed to prove black people inferior. They encouraged black people to learn to read and write so they could learn about their African heritage. They felt proud of their African past, seeing the glories and contributions of Africa as proof that black people were as capable as anybody in science, scholarship, civilization, and culture. As Berlin said, "They adamantly proclaimed their American nationality, but the motherland had undeniable pull. Free Negroes—of all denominations—called their churches 'African churches,' their schools 'African schools,' and their benevolent societies 'African benevolent societies.'"[12] They developed a race lexicon. Hence, the language of the race conscious was peppered with favorable talk about "champions of the race," "racial watchdogs," "racial uplifters." They spoke favorably of blacks who were a "credit to the race" and unfavorably of "race traitors," "race peddlers," and blacks who "sold the race out."

If blacks educated themselves and carried themselves in a decorous manner, they were thought to be a credit to the entire race, but if they engaged in crime or drank habitually, they were ostracized as a blight on the race and accused outright of bringing down the entire black race. For free black race men and race women, the individual had to carry on his or her shoulders the burdens and glories

of the entire race, and, it was thought, the race progressed or stag-
nated according to the actions of each individual member of the race.
Therefore, in instilling racial pride in young blacks and in raising and
educating them to be a credit to their people, race men and race
women taught young blacks to emulate such people as Frederick
Douglass, who said, "I never rise to speak before an American audience without something of the feeling that my failure or success will
bring blame or benefit to my whole race."[13]

The racial consciousness and racial pride of free blacks
were not so limiting that they fixed blacks in a world that was exclusive of the dominant American society. Thus, as Sweet maintained,

> [Blacks] combined the two distinct but harmonious themes. . . .They
> asserted both their identity as blacks and their identity as Americans.
> At the same time that Blacks were nationalistic in their pride of color,
> pride of Black capabilities, and pride of culture which was free of the
> moral imperfections of the broader American society, they were na-
> tionalistic about the superiority of American ideals, their stature as
> Americans, and their rights as citizens of the American nation."[14]

INSTITUTIONALIZATION OF BLACK CAREGIVING

The racial consciousness of free black people made for
the institutionalization of the black helping tradition. It is what largely
distinguishes caregiving by slaves from that of the free blacks. The
slaves had natural helping networks, such as the extended family and
fictive kin relations but, unlike the free blacks, they were not allowed
to build churches, fraternal orders, schools, and other organizations
that would institutionalize or structure their various self-help activities.
The institutionalization of caregiving among free blacks was evident
in their churches, benevolent societies and fraternal orders, mental and
moral-improvement efforts, and organized protests. The cooperation
among status groups and between the sexes that was demonstrated
in slavery also was significant in the institutionalization of caregiving
among the free blacks; however, free blacks were in a position to form
a social-class strata—not just status groups, as in slavery.

Extended Family

The primary institution for helping and caring among the
free blacks was the extended family. Family members helped one
another in countless ways—emotionally, materially, and spiritually.

Moreover, cooperation between men and women and among status groups and mutual aid in the extended family were enlarged by fictive kinship and racial consciousness to involve the entire free-black community. The socialization of children meant rearing them to concern themselves not only with the welfare and plight of their relations, but with the welfare and plight of black people in general—slave and free.

Religious Consciousness and the Institutional Black Church

The black church was second only to the black extended family as a care-giving institution in the free black community. Because of racial prejudice in the white churches and the need of free blacks for a refuge where they could meet and worship God in their own way, express common grievances, and be themselves, free blacks founded churches. These churches grew out of the extreme religious consciousness of slave and nonslave blacks.

Religious consciousness, like fictive kinship ties and racial consciousness, was a key mechanism for spreading black caregiving from the family to the community. Religious-conscious blacks saw Jesus Christ as the quintessence of the spirit of brotherhood and sisterhood—as the greatest caring, giving, and sharing role model to be found on earth. Their love of God and, more important, their belief in God's love for them, was the bulwark on which rested their thirst for freedom and their desire to help others to be free. Even when racist whites took the brotherhood out of Christianity and made it an instrument of slavery and oppression, the religion of free blacks and slaves taught them that slavery was an abomination in the eyes of God and that, one day, God, with all His fiery wrath, would destroy such a wicked institution.

The most explicit expression of the desire to be free and to free others can be found in the spirituals, which Frederick Douglass said "were tones, loud, long and deep, breathing the prayer and complaint of souls boiling over with the bitterest anguish. Every tone was a testimony against slavery, and a prayer to God for deliverance from chains."[15] It is no wonder then that the slaves sang:

> My Lord delivered Daniel,
> My Lord delivered Daniel,
> My Lord delivered Daniel,
> I know he can deliver me!

* * * * *

If I had my way,
O Lordy, Lordy
If I had my way,
If I had my way,
I would tear this building down.

* * * * *

Go down Moses, 'way down in
Egypt's land;
Tell Ole pharoah
Let my people go![16]

Religious consciousness went hand in hand with and reinforced racial consciousness. Free blacks who were active in the cause of the social uplift of black people and in caregiving believed that they were carrying out the will of God and following the examples of Jesus Christ. God was commonly referred to by them as the "God of the poor and the needy" or the "God of the oppressed." This religious consciousness gave race-conscious free blacks added courage and fortitude in their desire to free the slaves and to be totally free themselves. If, for example, religious and race-conscious blacks such as Frederick Douglass, Sojourner Truth, and Harriet Tubman did not feel that God was on their side, protecting them as they carried out His will in the battle against powerful and murderous odds, it is hardly likely that they would have pressed forward with such strength, courage, and audacity. This belief led free black leaders to warn whites that "unless you speedily alter your course, you and your country are gone! For God Almighty will tear up the very face of the earth."[17]

Also, free black preachers often helped black slaves gain and keep their freedom. For example, the Reverend Leonard A. Grimes, a free black, was caught rescuing slaves and spent two years at hard labor in the state prison at Richmond, Virginia.[18] But imprisonment did not curtail his activities. After he was released, he founded a church for fugitive slaves in Boston and obtained clothes, food, shelter, and jobs for them; hid them from slave catchers, and even raised money to buy their freedom.[19] Another black preacher, the Reverend Elijah Anderson of Indiana, "died in 1857 at a state prison in Frankfort, Kentucky, where he was serving a term for conducting fugitive slaves across the state line."[20]

Benevolent Societies and Fraternal Orders

Benevolent societies and fraternal orders, which emerged in the black churches, were significantly involved in providing aid and services to needy blacks. An early benevolent society, the Free African Society, was under the auspices of an early black-organized church— the African Methodist Episcopalian Church. The 1789 charter of the Free African Society stated, in part, that its members formed such an organization "to support one another in sickness, and for the benefit of their widows and fatherless children."[21] The constitution of the Brown Fellowship Society, organized in 1790, said:

> We, the free brown men of South Carolina, taking into consideration the unhappy situation of our fellow creatures, and the distress of our widows and orphans, for the want of a fund to relieve them in the hour of their distress, sickness and death; and holding it an essential of mankind to contribute all they can toward relieving the wants and miseries, and promoting the welfare and happiness of one another, do hereby organize ourselves into the Brown Fellowship Society of the city of Charleston.[22]

Benevolent societies became a distinguishing feature of practically all free Negro communities, particularly urban ones. For example, after the Free African Society was founded in Philadelphia in 1839, the number of such organizations grew so that by 1889, "Philadelphia had 80 mutual relief societies...and the number grew to 106 ten years later, enrolling one-half of the adult black population."[23]

The black community was so much better organized and equipped than the white community in Philadelphia for caregiving that the white community turned to the black community for salvation when Philadelphia was plagued by an epidemic of yellow fever in 1793. It was reported that "the hospitals were overflowing with victims, and even the doctors and nurses were falling prey to the stampeding epidemic."[24] In desperation, blacks were offered twice the going wages for nursing care and for the removal of bodies from the victims' homes. The newspapers carried stories of the medical reasons why blacks could not be infected with the dread disease and printed stories of love and praise for those blacks who volunteered their services. The leaders of the Free African Society—the Reverend Richard Allen and the Reverend Absolom Jones—were confused about the position they should take because they realized that, despite what many whites believed, blacks were not immune to the disease.[25] Nevertheless, these leaders called for volunteers to aid their white brethren in the name of humanity, and a number of black lives were lost in that endeavor.[26]

Fraternal orders also became numerous after Prince Hall founded in 1787 what is now the oldest social organization among blacks in this country—the first black Masonic lodge. The black Masons and other fraternal orders had a reputation for their charitable activities. Both the benevolent societies and the fraternal orders provided a number of social services; they offered burial for their members, furnished disabled members with "weekly 'sick dues' to assure them an income while they could not work, gave pensions to elderly members and also to widows and children of dead members. . .ran schools for orphan children or apprenticed the children of deceased members to successful free Negro tradesmen," and furnished companionship for the sick and disabled by ordering all members to spend time with incapacitated members.[27] In addition, they set up associations like Baltimore's Society for Relief in Case of Seizure to guard against man stealers, "tried to secure better wages or a degree of job security in an era when free Negroes were being pushed out of a number of trades. . .worked to relieve the poor, support schools, send missionaries to Africa, or simply provide a place where friends might meet in good fellowship."[28] In these mutual-aid societies and fraternal orders, free Negroes provided relief designed to improve their lot even under the radically circumscribed milieu of racism.

Mental and Moral Improvement Efforts

Institutions designed to improve the mentality and morality of blacks were nearly as popular among free blacks as were their churches, benevolent societies, and fraternal orders. Indeed, the churches, mutual-aid societies, and fraternal orders were primary instruments in efforts toward this end. In seeking the moral and mental improvement of the race, free black leaders emphasized hard work, frugality, industriousness, education, sobriety, and similar virtues. They saw these virtues as the means to social uplift and respect and strongly believed that "self-improvement would in itself raise blacks from degradation."[29] According to Cooper,

> . . .degradation was ignorance, intemperance, menial jobs and improper conduct. The frequent use of works like "improvement," "elevating," "rising" conveyed the image of emerging from degradation to a "respectable," "useful," and "civilized" existence. Each black who conformed to respectable standards of conduct, improved his mind and worked hard was himself elevating the race.[30]

Although some free blacks sought membership in benevolent societies, fraternal orders, and other institutions to gain a higher status than other blacks and some saw the value they placed on hard work, frugality, sobriety, and morality as a mark of superiority to the black masses, many other free blacks considered themselves in the vanguard of the struggle to educate and uplift the people to whom they were tied by blood and common oppression. These free blacks stressed education as a tool for freedom. Therefore, they helped to build schools, literary societies, libraries, and debating clubs for what was referred to as the "mental improvement of the race."

Schools. Schools sprang up everywhere in free black communities because education was viewed almost as a religion. Blacks were urged to save their money, particularly by not spending it on gambling, drinking, and other vices, and to invest it in obtaining an education, if not for themselves, then for their children. The awareness that slaves were forbidden to learn how to read and write and that whites generally thought all blacks were mentally inferior motivated free blacks even more to learn. All the free black institutions placed a heavy emphasis on learning, and hardly any black leader could speak before a black audience without stressing the need for education. It was even thought that "social events could be put to educational purposes if young men would turn soirees into serious discussion groups to improve their own minds and those of their young ladies."[31]

The extreme importance placed on education was primarily aimed at getting blacks not to be content with being menials. During the eighteenth and nineteenth centuries, great black leaders were adamant that blacks should use education as a tool to rise above the status of "hewers of wood and drawers of water." The eighteenth-century black leader, James Forten, Jr., a wealthy shipbuilder, asked: "Shall we, when told that we aspire to no other station than hewers of wood and drawers of water, respond Amen, even be it so?"[32] And Maria Stewart asked black women: "How long shall the fair daughters of Africa be compelled to bury their minds and talents beneath a load of iron pots and kettles?"[33] She warned black women that they would never "enrich themselves by spending their lives as house-domestics, washing windows, shaking carpets, brushing boots, or tending upon gentlemen's tables."[34] Walker wrote: "I do not mean to speak against the occupations which we acquire enough and sometimes scarcely that, to render ourselves and families comfortable through life. . . . My objections are to our glorying and being happy in such low employment."[35] In a similar tone, Delaney, speaking vociferously against blacks seeking positions as "servants, waiting maids, coachmen, nurses, cooks in gentlemen's kitchens, or such like occupations," stated: "We have nothing to say against those whom necessity compels to do these things, those who can do no better; we have only to do with those who can, and will not, or do not do better."[36] Pease and Pease summarized these beliefs as follows:

> [The] argument was not that menial labor was, in itself, denigrating, for no "needful labor" was dishonorable; nor did any insist that blacks should never perform any kind of necessary and useful work. But, as the address of the Cleveland National Convention of 1848 made clear, "such employments have been so long and universally filled by colored men, as to become a badge of degradation, in that it has established the conviction that colored men are only fit for such employments."[37]

Temperance. If education was seen as the chief vehicle for mental improvement, temperance ranked high on the agenda of free blacks as a means of moral improvement. To many free blacks, sobriety was a mark of good moral character as well as a way to elevate the race. Therefore, temperance societies were as widespread and as much a standard fixture of the free Negro community as were the benevolent societies and the churches. There were the Daughters of Temperance and the Sons of Temperance, the Temperance Society of People of Color, and so forth.[38] Blacks who were active in these movements strongly believed that the excessive use of alcohol would retard the progress of the race. They also associated alcohol with crime, delinquency, idleness, family instability and those "scenes of iniquity, the gaming table, the brothel and the theatre, 'where blacks wasted both their money and their souls.'"[39] Furthermore, they did not want black people to be stereotyped as a race of drunkards.

Protest. The institutionalization of protest was another means by which race-conscious free blacks sought to uplift and advance the race. Although the free blacks in the South could not openly protest the plight of black people as could free blacks in the North, and those blacks in the rural areas could not be as vociferous in their protest as those in the larger towns and cities, protest among free blacks was strong everywhere. Although the abolition of slavery was the primary goal of free blacks, they fought also for the right to vote, for civil rights, for equality, inclusion, and justice. The participation of free blacks in the Underground Railroad and the abolitionist movement has already been mentioned. When the Fugitive Slave Law of 1850 was passed, free blacks created numerous organizations to fight against what they called "manstealing." As Quarles noted, "defiance of the Fugitive Slave Law became a new commandment to abolitionists throughout the North;...up to 1850 the rescuing of fugitive slaves had been a business conducted almost exclusively by Negroes."[40]

Free blacks also made extensive use of the petition as a political instrument. They took every opportunity to sign petitions expressing their grievances against slavery and other indignities suffered by black people. Indeed, free blacks made such extensive use of this instrument of protest that a petition, aimed at freeing a runaway slave, which was sent to a congressman in Washington in 1842, bore 51,862 signatures. The petition was on "an immense roll of paper the size of a barrel."[41] A petition sent to the Massachusetts legislature in 1843 bore 61,526 signatures and weighed 150 pounds.[42]

Another major protest weapon used by free blacks was the Negro conventions. In these conventions, free blacks could argue, debate, and reach agreements on courses of actions and priorities for elevating the race and freeing it from bondage. These conventions allowed blacks to rebuke the alleged inferiority of black people, laud the achievements of blacks, praise black heroes and heroines, release pent-up emotions, train and demonstrate black leaders, and reinforce their commitment to ending slavery and becoming first-class citizens.

ROLE OF WOMEN

Black women assumed major functions in the helping institutions of the free blacks. They played an economic role that was indispensable to the survival of the extended black family. That women had to work if the family was going to survive made it easier for them to take their rightful place and to be accepted as the equals of men. In the abolitionist movement, black women abolitionists, such as Frances Ellen Watkins, Sojourner Truth, and Charlotte Forten, were staunch advocates of the equal rights of women and "on the whole during the antebellum period, black male leaders were more sympathetic to women's rights than white male leaders."[43]

Black women had suffered every trial black men had suffered and they were not about to accept full freedom for black men and semi-freedom for themselves. Quarles stated that "black women were among the first women in America to sit down with their men around political matters."[44] Therefore, in abolitionist societies and other black organizations, women generally played a significant part. Even the fraternal orders had auxillary units for women. As precarious as was the condition of black people, free black women and free black men were inclined to see it necessary for men and women to work together in a common struggle. Even when black men wavered and succumbed to the male chauvinism predominant in the society, black women refused to be relegated to an inferior place. The matriarch of the black race, Sojourner Truth, said: "I feel that if I have to answer for the deeds done in my body just as much as a man, I have a right to have just as much as a man."[45] This was the general mood of women in the free black community.

Even in male-dominated institutions such as the black church and black fraternal orders, women played a significant role. They were the backbone of the black church, and the all-male fraternal orders depended on them to raise funds for many charitable activities. Their role as fundraisers explains why many black fraternal orders had auxillary or umbrella women's groups.

Overall, although free black men could not escape the male chauvinism characteristic of their day, race-conscious free black men seemed to have understood that the advancement of the race required the work, energy, and talents of both men and women. Hence, Delaney, a prominent black historical figure of the nineteenth century, expressed a common belief of both free black men and women when he wrote that "no people are elevated above the condition of their females;" like many other black male reformers and leaders, Delaney called for the education of black women so they could rise above being "washerwomen, chamber-maids, children's travel nurses, and common house servants, and menials," and take their rightful place beside black men in working to uplift and advance black people.[46]

Even if many black men took on the male-chauvinist attitudes of their white counterparts, black women generally were not about to be relegated to a position of inferiority after having been the black man's equal in slavery for so long and after having become his indispensable economic and political partner in freedom. Maria Stewart, who "may have been the first black woman to make a public statement on behalf of black advancement," issued the call many black women in those times were to take up.[47] She said, "O' ye daughters of Africa, awake! Awake! Arise!"[48]

REFERENCES

1. For an excellent discussion on the plight of free blacks, see Leon F. Litwack, *North of Slavery* (Chicago: University of Chicago Press, 1961); and Ira Berlin, *Slaves without Masters* (New York: Pantheon Books, 1974).

2. W. E. B. Du Bois, *Black Reconstruction in America: 1860–1880* (New York: Russell & Russell, 1935), pp. 10–11.

3. Ibid., p. 10.

4. Quoted in Benjamin Quarles, *Black Abolitionists* (New York: Oxford University Press, 1969), p. 6.

5. Berlin, *Slaves without Masters,* pp. 269–270.

6. William F. Cheek, *Black Resistance Before the Civil War* (Beverly Hills, Calif.: Glencoe Press, 1970), p. 19.

7. Berlin, *Slaves without Masters,* p. 42.

8. See Earl Conrad, *Harriet Tubman* (Washington, D.C.: Associated Publishers, 1943).

9. Quarles, *Black Abolitionists,* pp. 133, 135.

10. Herbert G. Gutman, *The Black Family in Slavery and Freedom, 1750–1925* (New York: Pantheon Books, 1976), pp. 216–217.

11. For a discussion on the concept of "race man" and "race woman," see St. Clair Drake and Horace Cayton, *Black Metropolis* (New York: Harcourt, Brace & World, 1945), pp. 394–395.

12. Berlin, *Slaves without Masters,* p. 158.

13. Frederick Douglass, *Life and Times of Frederick Douglass* (1881; New York: Collier Books, 1962), p. 376.

14. Leonard T. Sweet, *Black Image of America, 1784–1870* (New York: W. W. Norton & Co., 1976), p. 175.

15. Quoted in John Lovell, Jr., *Black Song: The Forge and the Flame* (New York: Macmillan Co., 1972), p. 228.

16. Ibid., pp. 234, 327, and 226, respectively.

17. David Walker, *An Appeal to the Colored People of the World* (Reprint, New York: Arno Press, 1969), p. 51.

18. William J. Simmons, *Men of Mark* (1887; Reprint, New York: Arno Press), p. 662.

19. Ibid., p. 663.

20. Quarles, *Black Abolitionists,* pp. 148, 162.

21. Sidney Kaplan, *The Black Presence in the Era of the American Revolution, 1770–1800* (Washington, D.C.: Smithsonian Press, 1973), pp. 84, 181.

22. Ibid.

23. Quarles, *Black Abolitionists,* p. 101.

24. Brenda Johnston, *Between the Devil and the Sea* (New York: Harcourt Brace Jovanovich, 1974), p. 67.

25. Ibid., p. 68.

26. Ibid.

27. Berlin, *Slaves without Masters,* pp. 307–309.

28. Ibid.

29. Frederick Cooper, "Elevating the Race: The Social Thought of Black Leaders, 1827–1850," *American Quarterly,* 24 (December 1972), pp. 604–625.

30. Ibid.

31. Jane H. Pease and William H. Pease, *They Who Would Be Free* (New York: Atheneum Publishers, 1974), p. 127.

32. As quoted in ibid., p. 132.

33. Quoted in Bert James Loewenberg and Ruth Bogin, *Black Women in Nineteenth-Century American Life* (University Park: Pennsylvania State University Press, 1976), p. 189.

34. Ibid., p. 193.

35. Walker, *An Appeal to Colored People,* p. 41.

36. Martin Delaney, *The Condition, Elevation, Images and Destiny of the Colored People of the United States of America Politically Considered* (1852; Reprint, New York: Arno Press, 1969), p. 199.

37. Pease and Pease, *They Who Would Be Free,* p. 126.

38. Quarles, *Black Abolitionists,* pp. 93–100.

39. Pease and Pease, *They Who Would Be Free,* p. 126.

40. Quarles, *Black Abolitionists,* p. 204.

41. Ibid., p. 193.

42. Ibid., p. 195.

43. Rosalyn Terborg-Penn, "Black Male Perspectives on the Nineteenth Century Woman," in S. Harley and Terborg-Penn, eds., *The Afro-American Woman: Struggles and Images* (Port Washington, N.Y.: Kennikat Press, 1978), p. 177.

44. Quarles, *Black Abolitionists,* p. 178.

45. Quoted in Loewenberg and Bogin, *Black Women,* p. 236.

46. Delaney, *The Condition, Elevation, Images,* p. 199.

47. Loewenberg and Bogin, *Black Women,* p. 183.

48. Ibid., p. 187.

3 THE HELPING TRADITION DURING RECONSTRUCTION

The Civil War had a devastating impact both on slave families and on free black families. Black life was disrupted, and the future of black people depended on the outcome of the war. Both slaves and free blacks sought their long-awaited freedom by joining or following the liberators from the North—the Union troops. They came to the Union army in all types of conditions; some came garbed in rags or with no shoes on their bleeding feet while others came naked, and many were afflicted with disease, wounded, hungry, and homeless. They came by the thousands and were placed either in "freedmen's villages" or "contraband camps," for they were considered to be contraband of war. There were pregnant women and homeless children and old people, all of whom were bewildered by the swift turns their lives were taking and by the horror of death. Yet still they came, driven by an unquenchable thirst to be free.

They came seeking freedom, but they often met prejudices against their color more bitter than any they had left behind. "To belittle the slave's character, dress, language, name and demeanor, to make him the butt of their humor, to ridicule his aspirations, to mock his religious worship, to exploit his illiteracy were ways of passing the duller moments of camp life and military occupation."[1] Black women were particularly subjected to barbarous treatment in these camps, as is illustrated by the following account of an incident involving soldiers stationed in Virginia:

> After seizing two "nigger wenches," they "turned them upon their heads and put tobacco, chips, stocks, lighted cigars and sand into their behinds." Without explanation, some Union soldiers in Hanover County,

49

Virginia, stopped five young black women and cut their arms, legs and backs with razors.[2]

Black womanhood was debauched, but black manhood asserted itself in ways never before expressed in this country. The war restored in black men the African warrior tradition that slavery had destroyed. And now that they were warriors again, helping the Union to win the war, and fighting with a passion and gallantry that shocked white people, North and South, they were, for the first time since their arrival in this country, not being called stupid, lazy, cowardly, and immoral by whites, but were instead being praised. One Yankee newspaper, the *New York Herald,* wrote that "these Negroes never shrink, nor hold back, no matter what the order. Through scorching heat and pelting storms, if the order comes, they march with prompt, ready feet...Such praise is great praise, and it is deserved."[3] General Stanton, the secretary of war, wrote in a letter to President Lincoln that "they have proved themselves the bravest of the brave, performing deeds of daring and shedding their blood with a heroism unsurpassed by soldiers of any other race."[4] And, according to General Grant, the head of the Union Army, for this once-thought-to-be handkerchief-headed, happy-go-lucky, shuffling, Sambo-type buffoon, "the problem is solved. The Negro is a man, a soldier, a hero."[5]

Du Bois, the black sage, was baffled. He wrote:

How extraordinary, and what a tribute to ignorance and religious hypocrisy, is the fact that in the minds of most people, even those of liberals, only murder makes men. The slave pleaded; he was humble...and the world ignored him. The slave killed white men; and behold, he was a man![6]

The war finally ended and in great jubilation the slaves sang:

Shout, O children!
Shout, you're free!
For God has brought you liberty!

* * * * *

Slavery chain done broke at last!
Broke at last! Broke at last!
Slavery chain done broke at last!
Gonna praise God till I die![7]

The slaves were free at last. But what a peculiar kind of freedom it was. True, the slave was free, remarked the great black emancipator, Douglass, but

...he had none of the conditions for self-preservation or self-protection. ...He was free from the individual master, but the slave of society. He had neither money, property, nor friends. He was free from the old plantation, but he had nothing but the dusty road under his feet. He was free from the old quarter that once gave him shelter, but a slave to the rains of summer and the frosts of winter. He was, in a word, literally turned loose, naked, hungry, and destitute, to the open sky.[8]

The condition of the newly emancipated slaves was so appalling that the black helping tradition had to be stretched to the limit to help reconstruct lives broken by slavery and devastated by war. Yet, patriarchy—the antithesis of black caregiving—gained greater prominence than ever in the black community.

PATRIARCHY

Black men, having passed what is universally considered by men to be the true test of manhood—the ability to kill other men— were beginning to feel more and more that they had earned the right to be the masters over their families and over black women, a so-called right of which slavery had deprived them. Many male house slaves and mulattoes had imitated the family patterns of their masters during slavery; in freedom, they wanted to outdo their former masters in establishing a patriarchy and prove that, by ruling the family system, they, too, were men. Now that former slaves could legally get married, many men took marriage to mean that they had legal dominance over black women and the religious vows requiring wives to honor and obey their husbands to mean that God "Himself" had sanctioned such dominance.

As patriarchy began to spread, it was only a short time before it became firmly rooted in a basic institution of the black community—the black church. The black church soon became a stronghold of patriarchy in which many black male preachers ruled supreme, becoming autocratic and dictatorial.[9] Quarles pointed out that the pre-Civil War black church, receiving its money from blacks and independent of white control, "could speak out on such issues as slavery without fear of losing members and offending someone in the South."[10] But, according to the theologian, Washington, "in the era of decline in the quest of freedom, the Negro minister remained the spokesman for the people with this difference—faced by unsurmountable obstacles, he succumbed to the cajolery and bribery of the white power structure and became its foil. Instead of freedom, he preached morality and emphasized rewards in the life beyond."[11] Another theologian, Cones, had a similar view of post-Civil War black ministers:

> The black ministers received personal favors from white society. Their churches were left alone. As long as blacks preached "about heaven and told Negroes to be honest and obedient, and that by and by God would straighten things out," whites supported black churches by lending them money to build new structures. . . . And the black ministers served them well.[12]

The chief danger of patriarchy at this critical moment in history was that it pitted black men against each other in a competitive economic effort, particularly the acquisition of status and material things; it called for the submission of black women to the power and authority of black men; and, overall, its emphasis was on having black men and black women seek social status and invidious distinctions instead of mutual survival and social change.

In the pre-Civil War free black communities, patriarchy on a smaller scale had already caused some black men who could support their families to form alliances against those who could not, and it had led some black men to use churches, fraternal orders, and education not so much for helping as for creating social distance. These practices of class divisiveness became more pronounced among black men after the war, particularly among black men who had managed to acquire property.

But although patriarchy was becoming entrenched in the black community, it did not stop the massive self-help endeavors of black people. The condition in which black people found themselves after the Civil War and emancipation provided them with one of the greatest and severest tests of the helping tradition that had been cultivated in Africa, retained and sharpened in slavery, and institutionalized in free black communities.

BLACK CAREGIVING DURING RECONSTRUCTION

The Bureau of Refugees, Freedmen and Abandoned Lands, popularly known as "The Freedmen's Bureau," was instrumental in providing clothing, shelter, medical care, tools, land, and education to thousands of emancipated blacks. Many white philanthropists and white organizations, such as the predominantly white American Missionary Association, worked hand in hand with the Freedmen's Bureau and managed to achieve a record of accomplishments in feeding, educating, clothing, and sheltering poor blacks and whites. But blacks did not stand idly by while the government and whites "did" for them. They were filled with a sense of mission to free their own brothers and sisters from wretchedness, disease, and ignorance.

Magdol held that mutuality was so strong among the ex-slaves that it evidenced itself early in the contraband camps and freedmen's villages.[13] Blacks, anxious to prove that they were worthy of full-fledged American citizenship and that they could be independent of any white master, cooperated enthusiastically in building homes, schools, churches, and roads, and even demonstrated capabilities in self-government. This mutuality, Magdol held, was "a synthesis of African and Euro-American cultural components" centered "in great part on kinship, an extended family extended to a plantation, a camp, a village."[14]

Funds from the Masses

Never before had the masses of poor, ignorant, broken black people expressed such zeal about uplifting themselves. Albion W. Tourgee held that during the Reconstruction period, poor, half-starved blacks "paid a larger proportion of their income for charitable and religious purposes than any people known to history."[15] Indeed, because the black populace had such small upper, middle, and professional classes, the funding of black churches, old-folks' homes, orphanages, and so forth depended on the nickle-and-dime donations of the mass of illiterate, impoverished black people. For example, Mary C. Fleming, a schoolteacher in Lawford, Virginia, obtained donations from her impoverished students to be sent to an orphans' home. She wrote the following letter to the director of the home:

> I decided that I would take up a few pennies in my school or as much as I could among my scholars and myself. I asked them if they were willing to send something to the orphan home and they agreed with me. Though small in amount, I hope it will be of some help to the good works. The following are the names and amounts. . .from the Peterville School House: Teacher, Mary C. Fleming, 25¢; Ellen Hartwell, 5¢; Geneva Booker, 5¢; Florence Fleming, 5¢; Willie S. Allen, 5¢; Mary Wilson, Cornelius Taylor, David Fleming, George Booker and Jack Toney all 5¢.[16]

Care for the Old and the Young

A great portion of these contributions went into the care of the elderly; building homes for old blacks, Du Bois documented, became "the most characteristic Negro charity."[17] "Next to homes for the aged," Du Bois went on, "the Negroes...felt the need of orphanages and refuges for children" because slavery and the Civil War had left thousands of black children parentless and homeless."[18] Moreover, the built-in mutual-aid system in the black extended family brought thousands of family members to the rescue of both kin and nonkin alike, helping men with no means of support, women with no husbands, old folks with no place to go, and children with no parents. As Gutman wrote:

> Obligation toward nonslave kin was most powerfully expressed during and after the Civil War in the attention ex-slaves gave the black children orphaned by the sale and death of their parents, by paternal desertion, and by wartime dislocation. The exact number of orphans can never be known. Some were absorbed into extended kin groups, and others found places with non-kin. Blacks called them "motherless children," and ex-slaves shared "a beautiful charity" to these poor orphan children, even though starvation may [have stared] them in the face.[19]

Benevolent Societies and Fraternal Orders

The benevolent societies, fraternal orders, and secret societies that had previously addressed themselves largely to the needs of free blacks in the pre-Civil War period were reactivated to deal with the hordes of needy and destitute emancipated slaves and, once again, they became ubiquitous in the black community. The benevolent societies later formed the basis of the first black insurance companies and, of course, became motivated more by a desire to make money than to give it away to charitable endeavors. Later, the fraternal orders became more exclusive and bourgeois. But, during the Reconstruction period, the benevolent societies and the fraternal orders were in their highest historical stage of caring for ex-slaves and other destitute blacks.

Black Philanthropy

In addition to benevolent societies and fraternal orders, there were individual black philanthropists all over this country, despite the pervasive poverty among the black majority. Some black philanthropists, such as Colonel Lafon of New Orleans and Biddy Mason of Los Angeles, gave thousands of dollars to charitable causes. The time of slavery had its black philanthropists too. For example, "Mammy" Pleasant funded John Brown's raid at Harpers Ferry, Virginia, to the tune of $30 thousand. However, it was the Reconstruction period that totally awakened black philanthropy. During that period of crisis, one did not have to be wealthy to be a philanthropist. Many blacks were known to bequeath whatever money was left after their funeral expenses to charitable causes, and however little was given was greatly appreciated. Whites were philanthropists when they gave thousands or sometimes millions of dollars, but blacks, because of their general destitution, were philanthropists when they gave nickels and dimes.

Social-Class Cooperation

Black philanthropy indicates that the social-class and status-group cooperation inherent in black extended families was still strong during the Reconstruction period. Probably never before or since have the different social classes and status groups cooperated with such great enthusiasm as they did in the post–Civil War days. Lindsay affirmed this type of cooperation, which could be seen in black communities all over the country:

> During the severe depression of 1893, the more economically privileged members of the Negro group in Washington were aroused by the plight of their less fortunate fellow citizens. One of these was familiarly known as the "Hill group." Led by Mrs. Sara Fleetwood, the Hill group brought coal and large stores of staples such as lard, cornmeal, sugar and flour and supplemented these with potatoes, apples, and meat. These they stored in the Fleetwood home for issuance to the needy. Mrs. Fleetwood and her neighbors continued their relief activities throughout the depression of 1893.[20]

Education

One area in which the black social classes cooperated with great enthusiasm was education. Educated blacks cooperated with illiterate blacks for social uplift through education and were primarily responsible for creating and making black schools major institutions during the Reconstruction years. Aware that the newly free blacks were suffering from an incredible ignorance, the more educated blacks urged the black masses to get an education, and their urging met with positive results. Haynes, a founder of the National Urban League, wrote that "day-schools, night-schools, vacation schools, summer schools, and their limited colleges" were "always overcrowded" during the Reconstruction period as blacks were moved by an extraordinary desire to throw off the yokes of ignorance.[21]

Women's Club Movement

Another area that demonstrated cooperation between the social classes for mutual aid was the rise of the women's club movement. The late nineteenth century produced some of the greatest black women in Afro-American history: Fannie M. Barrier, Nannie Helen Burroughs, Anna J. Cooper, Fannie Coppin, Mary Church Terrell, and Ida B. Wells, to name a few. These women, and thousands of others like them, made a fervent plea for black women to maintain their stand as equals. "For woman's cause is man's," wrote Anna J. Cooper. "They rise or sink together, dwarfed or godlike, bond or free."[22]

These black women were active in two major black institutions—the school and the women's club. If men dominated the church, black women and white women took on the herculean task of trying to educate a people with an illiteracy rate of 95 percent, and they were largely successful in teaching millions of former slaves to read, write, and do basic arithmetic. In the women's clubs, more privileged black women worked together with their not-so-privileged black sisters. Josephine St. Pierre Ruffin, a pioneer in the women's club movement and founder of the New Era Club of Boston, came from a privileged background, as did Mary Church Terrell. Yet these women, like others of their class, were deeply committed to advancing black people on the whole, regardless of social class or status, and to relating to all black women as their sisters. They stated categorically: "We are not a set of butterflies on dress parade. Most of our club women are the best housekeepers, the best wives and the best cooks; yet we are the most self-sacrificing women, ever on the alert to relieve suffering humanity."[23] Their pledge was the promise to stand "united for God, ourselves, and our race"; their motto, the words "lifting as we climb"; and their most basic belief, that a people "can rise in the scale no higher than its womanhood."[24]

The women's club became an important black charitable organization. Women's club members established day nurseries and kindergartens for children of working mothers; gave out shoes, clothing, milk, and medical care to needy children; and set up institutions or raised money to care for the orphaned and the aged. They helped unattached young girls find decent lodging and social activities that would keep them from the vicious world of the streets; started programs to rescue "fallen women"; and raised funds and fought for reformatories for juvenile delinquents. Also, they organized savings plans for black women to set aside money toward buying homes; counseled and gave assistance to expectant mothers; held classes in homemaking, child care, hygiene, and health care; led antituberculosis campaigns and temperance campaigns, and visited prisons. In addition, they set up literary and reading societies; raised funds for and created schools; and held conferences at which they explained the plight of black people, mapped out programs for black advancement, and re-affirmed their commitment to the cause.[25]

So active were black women in charitable work among their people that they produced such pioneers in social welfare as Catherine Ferguson, one of the first persons to establish homes for destitute and homeless children. Women's clubs were said to be "second only to the church in influencing the establishment of welfare services for the race."[26] But in terms of black caregiving, the extended family ranked first, the black church ranked second, and the women's clubs ranked third.

The Black Extended Family

The black extended family on which the helping tradition rests was still the dominant care-giving institution in the black community during Reconstruction. The tenancy–share-cropping system, which was instituted to revive a bankrupt southern agriculture, subjugated blacks to a form of neoslavery. This system was so destructive to the interests of blacks that black people often had no choice but to depend on relatives for support to survive it. The tenancy–share-cropping system, which claimed the lives of so many blacks during that era, helped organize scattered black individuals and families and, to some extent, helped stabilize the black community by again giving it economic roots in the soil. But the system required that black people work like mules for scanty wages (if they ever received the wages due to them); often, the harder they worked, the more they became indebted to many of the same white men who were once their slave masters.

Black men who were seeking a new day for themselves and their families generally found themselves returned to a position of powerlessness. All too soon, they found that the heroism they displayed in helping to save the Union would not result in their sharing patriarchal authority and power with white men. Again they were looked on as being lazy, shiftless "niggers" who had literally to be starved to be made to go to work. Once again, they could not protect their women and children from the abuse and brutality of white men. And if they fought back, the lynch rope all too often found its way around their necks.

Black men could pretend they were patriarchs in the black family. But this pretense often created more male-female friction than anything else, particularly since black men depended on the labor and wages of their women and, unlike men of means, were unable to reward their women for taking a subordinate role. As Cox wrote:

"When freedom came, this tradition of the Negro woman as a worker continued. The Negro wife tended to continue her traditional work outside the home, and the husband ordinarily showed that he expected her to do so."[27] As it did in slavery, the extended family rebelled against patriarchy and matriarchy, as well as against antagonistic, competitive social classes as it sought to rely on men and women—both the well-off and the downtrodden—for the mutual survival of the family in a hostile American Society.

RECONSTRUCTION: SUCCESSES AND FAILURES

The women's clubs, the black church, the black extended family, and other helping institutions worked together to meet two of the greatest challenges presented to black people in this country: To reconstruct lives twisted and debased by slavery and war and to move an illiterate, impoverished people from slavery to citizenship. These institutions met with some success. Thousands of blacks were fed, clothed, cared for medically, and sheltered; thousands of them broke the yokes of illiteracy in hundreds of schools, including black colleges, that sprang up everywhere; and black people had shown that they were among the great survivors in this country. The most significant success that black caregivers could claim during this critical juncture in history was that they helped many blacks to overcome the extreme alienation that comes from years of oppression and isolation and from being perennially treated like outsiders. These caregivers tried to show black people their worth and potential and to get black people to feel pride and hope even in the midst of enduring oppression and despair. Furthermore, they tried to get blacks to rid themselves of their dependence on white masters and of the Uncle Tom, "good-old-darkey" leadership and to rely on all the self-help lessons they had learned in Africa and in slavery.

In seeking to face the historical challenge presented by war, emancipation, and Reconstruction, the black caregivers demonstrated that black life in this country has continuity; it has a foundation in the past—a helping spirit to be passed on to future generations. However, although the helping tradition reached a peak during the Reconstruction period, it was overwhelmed by forces largely outside its control. The reconstruction of black life and white life and the overall rebuilding of this country was a failure.

Blacks learned a painful lesson during that period. They learned that their freedom was still not totally in their own hands, that full first-class American citizenship still depended on the willingness of white people to live up to the democracy that was easily professed. They learned that despite their great effort to uplift themselves, they still could not fully overcome the shadows of the plantation—disease, ignorance, poverty, and racism—conditions that promised to plague black people for at least another century.

After slavery, blacks wanted land, equal protection under the law, the right to vote, economic security, and education—first-class American citizenship, in other words. The Fifteenth Amendment gave blacks (black men, that is) the right to vote, and the Northern troops stationed in the ex-confederate states gave the newly freed blacks some protection from the bitter, vengeful whites, which made it possible for black people to participate in politics to a degree unprecedented in black American history. But black people were betrayed by the Republican party, by Northern industrialists, and by President Rutherford B. Hayes's bargain to remove the Northern troops from the South and allow the white Southerners to write their own state constitutions. Thus, what started out as an extraordinary move toward real democracy in this country ended with black elected officials being stripped of power and thrown out of office and black voters being terrorized at the polls or being deprived of their right to vote by such unfair, racist requirements as the "grandfather clause." These times became, for blacks, one of lynching, Jim Crow legislation, Black Codes, Ku Klux Klan terrorism—of efforts to relegate blacks to an inferior status only a notch or two above slavery.

REFERENCES

1. Leon F. Litwack, *Been in the Storm So Long* (New York: Alfred A. Knopf, 1979), p. 128.

2. Ibid., p. 130.

3. Quoted in W. E. B. Du Bois, *Black Reconstruction in America: 1860–1880* (New York: Russell & Russell, 1935), p. 110.

4. Quoted in Benjamin Quarles, *The Negro in the Making of America* (New York: Collier Books, 1964), p. 119.

5. Quoted in Du Bois, *Black Reconstruction in America,* p. 111.

6. Ibid., pp. 104–110.

7. Quoted in John Lovell, Jr., *Black Song: The Forge and the Flame* (New York: Macmillan Co., 1972).

8. Frederick Douglass, *The Life and Times of Frederick Douglass* (1881; Reprint, New York: Collier Books, 1962) p. 377.

9. E. Franklin Frazier, *The Negro Church in America* (Reprint, New York: Schocken Books, 1963), p. 49.

10. Benjamin Quarles, *Black Abolitionists* (New York: Oxford University Press, 1969), p. 82.

11. Joseph R. Washington, *Black Religion* (Boston: Beacon Press, 1972), p. 35.

12. James H. Cones, *Black Theology and Black Power* (New York: Seabury Press, 1969), p. 69.

13. See Edward Magdol, *A Right to the Land: Essays on the Freedmen's Community* (Westport, Conn.: Greenwood Press, 1977), chapter 4, pp. 90–109.

14. Ibid., pp. 73, and 107.

15. Quoted in Herbert Gutman, *The Black Family in Slavery and Freedom, 1750–1925* (New York: Pantheon Books, 1976), p. 541.

16. William L. Pollard, *A Study in Black Self-Help* (San Francisco: R & E Associates, 1978), p. 110.

17. W. E. B. Du Bois, *Efforts for Social Betterment Among Negro Americans* (Atlanta, Ga.: Atlanta University Press, 1909), p. 65.

18. Ibid., p. 77.

19. Gutman, *The Black Family,* p. 227.

20. Inabel B. Lindsay, "The Participation of Negroes in the Establishment of Welfare Services, 1865–1900" (Ph.D. thesis, University of Pittsburgh School of Social Work, 1952), p. 66.

21. George Edmund Haynes, *The Trend of the Races* (Miami, Fla.: Minemosyne Publishing Co., 1976), p. 93.

22. Quoted in Bert James Loewenberg and Ruth Bogin, eds., *Black Women in Nineteenth-Century American Life* (University Park: Pennsylvania State University Press, 1976), p. 187.

23. Du Bois, *Efforts for Social Betterment Among Negro Americans,* p. 51.

24. Ibid., pp. 51–52.

25. Lindsay, "Participation of Negroes," pp. 168–186.

26. Ibid., p. 66.

27. Oliver C. Cox, *Race Relations* (Detroit: Wayne State University Press, 1976), p. 176.

4 THE BLACK HELPING TRADITION IN RURAL AND URBAN AMERICA

At the turn of this century, the black helping tradition was still prevalent in both rural and urban areas. The rigid segregation of blacks during that time ensured that the tradition would persist to a certain extent. Segregated from the dominant national life, blacks had no choice but to create care-giving institutions to help their needy and their distressed. This rigid segregation reinforced a strong sense of racial consciousness in blacks, and the turn of the new century saw the rise of racial uplift organizations such as the National Association for the Advancement of Colored People, the Universal Negro Improvement Association (Marcus Garvey's powerful organization), and the National Urban League, one of the first black organizations to use professional social workers to seek solutions to problems facing urban blacks. This period also gave birth to the black renaissance movement and to the call for a "New Negro" and a "talented tenth" to help blacks rise. The great sage, Du Bois, prophesized that the problem of the twentieth century would be the problem of the color line.[1]

Earlier social science studies verified the existence of the black helping tradition in rural areas and small towns. Johnson, in his study of several rural counties in Georgia, discussed the black helping tradition with respect to the church, the black extended family, and other black care-giving institutions.[2] Powdermaker observed the prevalence of what she called "intra-Negro charity" in her study of small-town blacks.[3] And Lewis, in his study of a small-town black community, examined the extended family as a survival technique and other mutual-aid organizations designed for black improvement and uplift.[4]

These studies saw the helping tradition largely as a response to racism and segregation. But Hill found it predominant as well in the all-black communities he studied in Oklahoma.[5] Moreover, Hill thought that the helping tradition in all-black communities was stronger than it was in the biracial communities studied by scholars such as Johnson and Powdermaker. "The underlying egalitarian ideology" that Hill said penetrated "the whole structure of all-Negro society" was expressed in such beliefs as "we're all alike here," "we don't have no classes," "everybody got the same opportunities here" and "there ain't no difference among us."[6] Hill's study is significant because it suggests that the black helping tradition goes deeper than just a basic response to racism.

The turn of the century also found the care-giving emphasis in black life strong in urban areas, although cities often are viewed as a destroyer of traditions. Du Bois, in his study of blacks in Philadelphia in the early part of the twentieth century, found that mutual-aid organizations were almost as prevalent then as they were in the nineteenth century when caregiving among black Americans reached unprecedented heights.[7] In addition to the old helping institutions, such as churches, benevolent societies, and fraternal orders, urban life among blacks in the early part of this century demanded new efforts at black social welfare. These new efforts included homes for wayward girls, to protect teenage black girls from the antisocial aspects of big-city life; the reformatory movement, to create reform schools to steer young people away from delinquent and criminal activities; and the alley-reform movement, to make alleys safer and more sanitary. In addition, the housing reform movement worked to get blacks out of the worst slums in the big city into better housing; the health reform movement, to improve the health and recreational needs of a people crowded into unsanitary tenements; the recreational reform movement, to create recreational centers and parks so black children would have safe places to play and wholesome activities to occupy them; and the labor union movement, to integrate racist labor unions and to fight for better jobs, better pay, and greater economic security. In a sense, all the movements to improve the quality of life of urban blacks were intertwined. They were related to blacks being black in a racist society and poor and propertyless in a capitalistic society. For example, the housing and health problems of urban blacks were inseparable. Most of the urban black poor were rigidly segregated and forced to live in dilapidated, dirty, unventilated, overcrowded tenements in which all kinds of diseases festered and that led to a high mortality rate.

A report put out by Du Bois in 1906 stated that, in 1890, the death rate per 1,000 living persons was 27.4 for black people and 19.5 for white people; in 1900, the figures were 25.3 and 17.3, respectively. For every 1,000 living black infants under one year old, 458 died in 1890 and 344 in 1900.[8] The leading cause of death for black people in 1890 and 1900 was tuberculosis, with pneumonia and nervous-system disorders close behind.[9] It was also found that 50 percent of every 100 cases of illness among blacks could have been prevented.[10] But in those days, hospitals and medical facilities not only discriminated against poor urban blacks, they barred black physicians and nurses. Blacks physicians and nurses even had to fight to be included in hospitals largely set up for black patients, such as Harlem Hospital in New York City and the Veterans Hospital in Tuskegee, Alabama. Therefore, the health movement in the black community was twofold. It involved fighting for the provision of better health care for urban blacks and for the inclusion of black medical professionals in medical settings.

DECLINE OF THE BLACK HELPING TRADITION

The black helping tradition, which was developed in traditional Africa and retained in slavery and that met the challenge well in the losing battle to reconstruct the lives of blacks fresh out of slavery and war, began to decline rapidly during the 1930s and has sunk nearly into insignificance today. The Great Depression of the 1930s and desegregation, which contributed greatly to the decline, will be discussed in Chapter 5. However, what is relevant to this chapter is our belief that the increased urbanization of blacks brought the black helping tradition for the first time into general conflict with the dominant values of white society. This conflict has nearly spelled the death-knell of the helping tradition in both rural and the urban black communities.

Rural-Urban Black Migration

In tracing the decline of the black helping tradition, it is necessary to go back to the rural and small-town areas and to follow the migration of rural and small-town blacks to urban centers. Blacks had been steadily trekking cityward since the turn of the century. World War I sparked a movement from every little hamlet, village, and backward area to the cities, where black people hoped to find a better life. The need of the war industry for cheap, unskilled laborers caught the attention of blacks who wanted to escape share-cropping and other semislavery types of work. Also, the heavy oppression of blacks in the rural and small-town areas of both the North and the South forced many to seek whatever freedom from harassment, intimidation, and victimization big-city life could offer. And some black newspapers, the *Chicago Defender* for example, urged blacks to leave the South, "the land of blight, of murdered kin, deflowered woman-hood, wrecked homes, strangled ambitions, make-believe schools, roving 'gun parties,' midnight arrests, rifled virginity, trumped up charges, [and] lonely graves, the land where every foot of ground marks a tragedy."[11]

The pattern of rural-to-urban migration generally is the same. First, blacks feel stifled by the drabness, the oppression, and the lack of opportunity in rural and small-town areas and seek a better life in the city. Second, they usually follow relatives who have paved the way. Members of rural extended families do not "want to be complete strangers in a world which can be vicious to the uninitiated."[12] Therefore, they move in with cousins, uncles, brothers, sisters, and aunts who migrated earlier and live with their relatives until they feel enough at ease in the city to go out on their own. Frazier thought that when migrants have been in the city for a while, they begin to shed the conventions and ways of their small-town existence and "become subject to all forms of suggestion to be found in the city."[13] But we found that the third stage of black migration involves the rural or small-town blacks in trying to resist the influence of big-city life.[14] They do so by trying to carve a small town out of the big city or to make the city smaller and thus more manageable. Therefore, their closest associates mainly are kin and friends from the same town. Often several blacks from the same town live on the same block, attend the same church, and "hang out" at the same "idling place" (a street corner, bar, or hangout where they gather largely to talk, play checkers, drink, gamble, and so forth). These small-town black migrants gather around extended family members and form "homegirl" and "homeboy" ties with others from their small town to assure their survival and to feel less alone, less a part of an impersonal world. And they seldom cut themselves adrift from their small-town moorings. As Grier and Cobbs held, small-town blacks can live in a city for 20 or 30 years and still consider their small-town origin their "home."[15] Moreover, many of them take advantage of every opportunity to return home to their people. When they die, their final resting place is likely to be their home town.

However, even when small-town black migrants attempt

to avoid the dominant influence of the big city, they generally are forced to succumb to it. First, they learn that many of their small-town ways do not fit in well in the big city. They are told by relatives and friends who have been in the city a while that city people are not to be trusted. They are told that city people are cold, "slick," and ever ready to pull a con game on their unsuspecting country cousins. They are told that you have to be suspicious of everybody. From this suspiciousness, they learn to put on a facade of toughness to ward off evil people who may try to do them harm. Second, they are constantly being told that their ways are "country." If they greet people, that is "country"; if they leave the door to their home or car unlocked, that is "country" too; and if they help somebody, particularly a stranger, that is "country" as well, for nobody is to be trusted.

The characterizing of small-town or rural blacks as "country" means that city-bred blacks or those who have been living in the city for a long time see these recent migrants as being unsophisticated and are inclined to ridicule the way they dress, talk, act, and think. It is not long before many of these recent migrants, despite themselves, seek more than anything else to rid themselves of being "country" so they can be acceptable. And, the only way not to be country is to dress, talk, act, and think like city folks—to take on their ways. Whatever communal spirit the recent migrants inherited in the small towns must be relinquished to a large extent if they are to gain acceptance and to survive big-city life.

The need to gain acceptance in the big city largely explains how the helping tradition started to decline with the increasing urbanization of black people. What happened was this: For the first time in Afro-American history, the helping tradition was not required for black people to survive. In traditional Africa, where people depended heavily on the precarious natural environment, helping one another was the key to survival; it was so important that it became a major factor in traditional African life. In slavery, the helping tradition was significant to black survival, and slavery actually reinforced the helping tradition. This was also the case during the Reconstruction period. Even in earlier periods when the urban black population was much smaller, black caregiving was viewed as necessary to help blacks adapt to and survive the hardships of the big city. But, as the urban black population grew, the black helping tradition came face to face with a world in which not helping people was considered to be more conducive to survival than helping them. And faced with the individualistic, secularistic, competitive thrust of the dominant urban values, the black helping tradition appeared to be an obsolete relic of the past; it appeared to be "country."

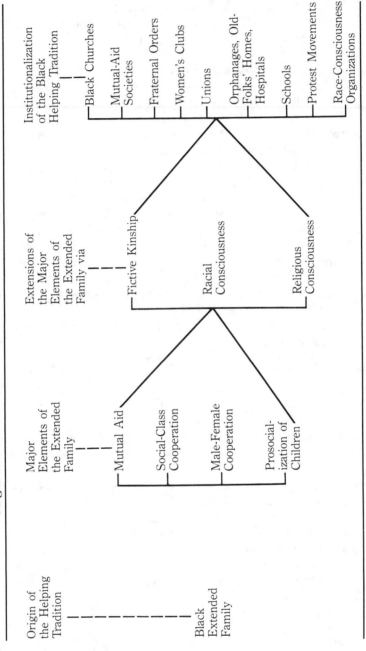

Fig. 1:
Origin and Institutionalization of the Black Helping Tradition

URBAN BLACK EXTENDED FAMILY

A crucial question that needs to be raised at this point is this: What about the black extended family? Is it not still essential to the survival of urban backs? The answer is yes. Even today, the extended family still plays a dominant role in the survival of black people in rural and urban areas. Without the black extended family, the prisons, nursing homes, foster homes, soup kitchens, and shelters for the poor in urban areas would be more crowded with blacks than they are now. The extended family assures thousands of jobless urban blacks the basic amenities of life. It informally adopts thousands of children whose parents cannot properly take care of them. It keeps thousands of elderly people from being unwanted and alone in the cities. And, in countless other ways, black kin aid one another in urban areas.

However, in earlier periods, the extended family played a much larger role in the development of care-giving institutions in the black community. The major elements of the extended family—mutual aid, social-class cooperation, male-female equality, and the pro-socialization of the children—were carried over into the larger black community by fictive kinship, racial consciousness, and religious consciousness. These major elements of the extended family gave rise to more black helping institutions—fraternal orders, mutual aid societies, and the like—that worked with the extended family for the survival of black people. Figure 1 presents a model of the helping tradition from its origin in the extended family to its institutionalization in the black community when the extended family played a greater role in the development of the helping tradition.

Today, the black extended family virtually stands alone as a care-giving institution created by black people for their survival in urban areas. The fictive kinship, racial consciousness, and religious consciousness necessary for transferring the major values of the extended family to the wider community have, for the most part, been checked by the individualistic, dog-eat-dog, competitive orientation of the dominant urban society.

Few urban blacks would put the welfare of nonkin and strangers on a par with that of kin. Strangers are not to be trusted. Furthermore, although racial consciousness is at a high level during critical moments in history, for example, during the 1960s, it tends not to be able to sustain the momentum necessary to become a sustaining influence in black urban life. Also, it was not structured in such institutions as black churches, schools, and the extended family. Urban blacks often see racial consciousness as detrimental to their desire to obtain money, jobs, and middle-class status and to assimilate into the dominant white culture. The overall desire of blacks to raise their individual social-class status takes priority over uplifting the entire race.

In the past, racial consciousness was what made the churches, fraternal orders, and other organizations consider the well-being of all black people—not just of their members. It was what made blacks go out of their way to help black strangers as if these strangers were kin. It was what moved many well-off blacks to give their time, energy, wisdom, and money to uplifting the masses of black people. It was what helped black men realize that the task of advancing black people was too herculean for them to take on without the help of black women. And it was what got the impoverished masses of blacks to dig deep into their pockets to find the nickels and dimes for charitable causes when they so sorely needed that money for themselves.

But the failure of blacks to institutionalize the black consciousness mood of the 1960s made it difficult to extend the helping tradition beyond the extended family and the isolated acts of black caregiving by churches and individuals. On the surface, it appears that religious consciousness is still strong in the urban black community, particularly because most cities have a large number of black churches. But as far as the black helping tradition is concerned, the proliferation of black churches in urban areas can be deceptive. Many churches have self-help programs to provide clothing and other needs. However, the black church, like the black extended family, is not able to check the growing individualism in the black community. It is unable to instill the Christian values of caregiving in urban blacks to the extent that it can raise the helping tradition to the high level of earlier periods or to the extent that it can play a significant role in combating crime, poverty, and racism in the black community.

The black church has been able to adapt to the individualistic, competitive orientation of the dominant urban culture by stressing an otherworldly stance that does not interfere with secular, worldly affairs. It has done so by adopting the Protestant-Calvinistic ethic of individualism and personal salvation that is consistent with the individualistic, pecuniary ethic of urban capitalism.

The Islamic religion also has been steadily growing in the urban black community. One of the five pillars of the Islamic religion is *zakāt* (charity). The following passage from the Koran is a clear example of Islam's emphasis on charity and mutual aid:

Worship none but God
Treat with kindness your parents and kindred
And orphans and those in need;
Speak fair to people;
Be steadfast in prayer;
and practice regular charity.[16]

It is too early to judge whether the Islamic faith will be any more successful than the Christian faith in reviving the black helping tradition.

The decline of the black helping tradition has been partly the result of the changing values of blacks, themselves. As they struggle to survive big-city life, black people have taken on values that call for "me first," instead of the "we first" law of traditional Africa and even slavery, and the dominant philosophy of "looking out for number one," instead of the African philosophy of "I am, because we are, and since we are, I am." Although the extended family still is necessary for the survival of black people in urban areas, it too has been eroded internally by the "me first" stance. For example, individualism threatens the value that the black extended family places on social-class cooperation by making well-off family members feel less obligated to the well-being of their impoverished kin. Even when children are socialized to take on the helping, caring, and sharing values of the extended family, they find that street life is hostile to those values, that the school system stresses the individualistic values of the dominant society, and that there are as many examples in the black community of people not caring for others as there are of people who help others. If the values of the extended family are not carried on by the younger generation, they will become extinct.

BOURGEOISIE IDEOLOGY AND STREET IDEOLOGY

The helping tradition in the urban black community is being supplanted by the bourgeoisie and street ideologies. These ideologies are similar in four ways. First, both place a great deal of emphasis on individualism. Second, both focus on obtaining money, material goods, and social status. Third, both are motivated by a desire to escape the hardships and the stigma of being poor. And fourth, by being consistent with the values of the status quo, both are supportive of the status quo. The two ideologies differ in that the bourgeoisie ideology stresses the use of legitimate means for individual uplift while the street ideology stresses the use of illegitimate means.

From Patriarchy to Bourgeoisie Values

The individualistic adaption of blacks to the city has become the dominant attitude of a number of hard-working, striving blacks who have managed to achieve middle-class status through legitimate means. Adopting a competitive, individualistic, Social Darwinistic stance, the efforts of these blacks are focused largely on improving their well-being and that of their immediate family and exclude most activities that involve helping other blacks.

In earlier generations, this stance was expressed by patriarchy. In strong patriarchal black families, the man was likely to view himself as an exceptional Negro—as the one out of a million who made it not by the help of others, he would claim, but by his own initiative and drive. Most significantly, he was likely to view himself as a man whose wife did not have to work, which was the general standard by which black men judged their success as patriarchs. He was apt to have no pity for those black men who had not "made it" or whose wives had to work outside the home. He was apt to be conservative and hostile toward helping other blacks or being helped by them, preferring to identify with and do the bidding of the white ruling class rather than to join oppressed black men and women in a common struggle.

Patriarchy and its attendant problems were not restricted to black families. It was the prevailing family form in this country. However, given the oppression of black people, it was especially pernicious among black families. In such rigidly patriarchal families, the woman played down her intelligence and her potential and took a "back seat" to her man, living for him and by his decisions. She showed off his wealth and status through the ostentatious display of such material goods as clothes, jewelry, and furniture; was his sex object; and made his life comfortable.

Children in such families grew up to take on an authoritarian personality.[17] They feared, yet respected and revered, the power of their fathers. They learned to establish hierarchical relationships with others and viewed people in terms of power and status rankings. They grew to despise weakness—the same weakness they saw in themselves and in their mother when they both submitted to the stern, demanding, dictorial father and husband. Their sibling rivalry became acute as they competed for their father's favor and approval and as they struggled to meet his competitive, status-seeking, acquisitive demands. Their identification with the ruling elite caused these children, as it did their fathers, to worship power, status, and authority. Furthermore, it fostered a hostile attitude toward the weak and the poor, a callousness and venality in the face of human suffering, and a zealous desire to mask their feelings of inferiority in the face of the raw power of white men by displays of ostentatiousness and conspicuous consumption. It was hardly likely that the black helping tradition would be instilled in or carried on by these children.

Today, the black middle class continues to increase in size because more and more black people are becoming professionals. Patriarchy has had to give way somewhat; well-off black men have realized that they can no longer boast about their wives' not having to work because both husbands and wives have to work if they are to maintain a middle-class standard of living. Also, middle-class black women, affected by the women's movement and more keenly aware of their historical tradition of equality with black men, have refused to be subordinated to black men.

Professional black men and black women, fulfilling equally important economic functions, are more economically self-sufficient, which has made it possible for them to form nuclear families. The nuclear families take on an egalitarian appearance. However, even when husbands in these nuclear families look on their wives as equals, it does not mean that they see other blacks—particularly poor or downtrodden blacks—in the same way. Nor does it mean that these husbands and wives use their joint income to help other blacks, even relatives, because members of nuclear families are generally concerned only with those in the narrow circle of their household. What it does mean is that these blacks are merely following the individualistic dictates to which all Americans are subjected. Thus, following consistently the norms of their society, these blacks are not required to, and are even encouraged not to, concern themselves with anybody but themselves. Contrary to Frazier's characterization of middle-class blacks as seeking to lose identification with the black masses, many middle-class blacks are actively involved in social change on behalf of all black people.[18] But these blacks are more consistently in tune with the demands of the black tradition than with the dictates of the general society.

Street Ideology

Poverty in the urban community makes blacks hungry for money. For many blacks who live in the squalors of the urban ghetto, getting money is the dominant motivating force in their lives. To have money means that they can escape the stigma and the hardships of poverty, and, they hope, acquire the middle-class standard of living by which success and worth are defined in this society. Many urban blacks seek to uplift themselves through education and professional pursuits, and many others try to advance by working hard. But there also are blacks who look past these alternatives, sometimes even frown on them, and seek to raise themselves by turning to the vicious world of the big-city streets.

To make it in the street life of the urban ghettoes, blacks must adopt the street ideology. This ideology requires them to display a dispassionate attitude that stresses exploiting, using, or conning others for economic, sexual, and ego gains. It requires that they be "cool." Being "cool" is a black ghetto phenomenon that is associated mainly with the street life of such black social deviants as gangsters, conmen, pimps, prostitutes, pushers, and "players." Cool blacks emphasize "rapping" (talking in a rhythmic manner, usually designed to use someone), "styling" (dressing fashionably and ostentatiously and driving new big or sports cars), "hustling" (making "fast" money through illegitimate means such as selling drugs, prostitution, numbers running, or running a con game), "fronting" (posing as sophisticated, tough, and flamboyant), "partying" (centering one's life on drinking, music, dancing, and taking drugs), and "getting over on people" (getting money, material things, and sexual gratification at the expense of others). These street blacks are in pursuit of the American Dream largely through illegitimate means that require the victimization of other black people.

Although they viciously prey on the black community, many urban black youths see cool or street blacks as role models because the cool lifestyle promises fast money, easy living, good times, and an identity. It does not matter that more often than not it leads to dead-end lives, prison, dope addiction, alcoholism, moral degradation, and early graves. Poor, badly educated or uneducated ghetto blacks who are stifled by unbearable poverty and oppression see street life as their only way out. And even the poor, nondeviant, hardworking, striving blacks —who make up the majority of ghetto dwellers —cannot escape been influenced by street people. Living in close proximity to street people, they find that the fear of being victimized or having actually being victimized by street blacks has caused them to take on a callous, suspicious, and negative attitude toward black people in general. Thus, when they are robbed, conned, or exploited by street blacks (and unscrupulous black bourgeoisies) their general attitude is, "Niggers ain't shit!"

It is easy to see that the street ideology is at variance with the black helping tradition. Helping, caring, and sharing, according to street blacks, are for "squares." With nondeviant blacks viewing other blacks with such suspiciousness and with many young blacks viewing cool blacks as role models and the street world as a way out, it is difficult for the helping tradition to survive.

The helping tradition has declined to such an extent that many social scientists studying ghetto life have come to see the street ideology and the cool lifestyle as the authentic black culture. Rainwater saw the cool lifestyle, or what he referred to as "expressive lifestyle," as the highest strategy that urban blacks have for survival and as "the crucible of black identity."[19] He defined this lifestyle as "an effort to make yourself interesting and attractive to others so that you are better able to manipulate their behavior along lines that will provide some immediate gratification."[20] Shultz, taking a lead from Rainwater, wrote that, in urban black areas, "playing it cool is a survival technique par excellence."[21] So important is playing it cool, he said, that the young ghetto boy is "ushered into the cool world by his mother," which means that "if the mother is to train her child for survival in the street, she must train him in the art of manipulation and deception," particularly in the art of how to manipulate and deceive black females.[22] For "in the cool world the ideal relationship (from the male's point of view) between the sexes is achieved by the man who 'pimps' his woman."[23] Thus, according to Shultz, so well is the boy in the ghetto taught to play it cool that, by the time he is a teenager, "the mother, who once was perceived as the source of all virtue, love, and dependability, must now be seen as a member of the opposite sex who is not to be trusted and indeed is someone to be 'put into a trick.' "[24] And a girl in the ghetto, Shultz said, becomes distrustful and defensive of cool men seeking to manipulate, deceive, and pimp her; nevertheless, she learns the necessity of "pleasing men." Thus, Shultz maintained, "for girls in their teens a choice must be made between planning a career (as typist, secretary, or nurse, for example) or 'doing it' with their boyfriend....The majority choose to 'do it.' "[25]

Keil's glamorization of the so-called expressive lifestyle is less crude than that of Shultz. Keil, like Rainwater, sees the expressive lifestyle in terms of symbolic or ritualistic action-feeling-body orientations, as opposed to thinking, rational, or mind orientations. Therefore, according to Keil, black culture is "predominantly auditory and tactile rather than visual and literate" and the difference between blacks and whites is "the prominence of aural perceptions, oral expression, and kinesic codes or body movement in Negro life."[26] According to Keil, it is entertainment, particularly black music, that is the soul and essence of the black culture and tradition, and it is the black entertainers, "singers, musicians, preachers, comedians, disc jockeys, some athletes and perhaps a few Negro novelists as well [who are the] identity experts [and] the ablest representatives of a long cultural tradition—what might be called the soul tradition."[27] Kiel predicted that a day would come when blacks "will cherish and defend this cultural identity, and they will see in their 'entertainers' the primary carriers of an irreplaceable tradition."[28]

Hannerz also was concerned with validating the cool lifestyle as an authentic black culture. He viewed the cool or expressive lifestyle as a ghetto-specific culture and listed its components as follows:

> ...female household dominance, a ghetto-specific male role of somewhat varying expression including, among other emphases, toughness, sexual activity, and a fair amount of liquor consumption; a relatively conflict-ridden relationship between the sexes; rather intensive participation in informal social life outside the domestic domain; and flexible household composition.[29]

Like Keil, Hannerz saw "the entertainers, preachers, disc jockeys, soul singers, emcees, and comedians" as the celebrants of "the cultural integration of the ghetto community."[30]

Without a doubt, the cool lifestyle receives its highest approval in *Rappin' and Stylin' Out*—which contains 27 articles that cover practically all the phases of the everyday world of cool.[31] Even the collection of articles edited by Rainwater in *Soul* cannot surpass *Rappin' and Stylin' Out* in seeking to legitimate the cool ideology and lifestyle as the authentic urban black culture.[32] The book even provides illustrations of how cool people walk, stand, and gesture when they put people in a "trick bag." Page after page presents the pimp, pusher, player, conman, and musician as the chief bearers of the black culture and tradition, and the attempt to legitimate the cool ideology and lifestyle is the thread that weaves together the collection of articles.

This social science perspective has been examined because it shows that some social scientists have come to see the street ideology as legitimate black culture when actually the street ideology is deviant from—the very antithesis of—legitimate black culture. The cool ideology rebels not only against the black helping tradition but against such major black traditions as religion and protest—traditions that blacks over the generations have deemed the key to the survival of black people in this country. Perhaps this social science perspective shows more than anything else the sharp decline of the helping tradition in urban America because the world presented in this perspective is not one of blacks helping one another as they have done since they arrived from Africa, but a world of blacks conning and manipulating one another. Moreover, because this perspective tends to be ahistorical, it portrays blacks conning and exploiting one another as the norm of black life in this country. It depicts the heroes and heroines not as race-conscious, religious-conscious, prosocial, helping oriented, selfless blacks, but as entertainers, the conmen, and those who play it cool.

REFERENCES

1. W. E. B. Du Bois, *Souls of Black Folk: Essays and Sketches* (1903; Reprint, Milwood, N.Y.: Kraus International Publications, 1973).

2. See Charles S. Johnson, *Shadow of the Plantation* (Chicago: University of Chicago Press, 1934).

3. Hortense Powdermaker, *After Freedom* (New York: Viking Press, 1939), p. 136.

4. See Hylan Lewis, *Blackways of Kent* (Chapel Hill: University of North Carolina Press, 1955).

5. Mozell Hill, "The All Negro Society in Oklahoma." Unpublished doctoral thesis, University of Chicago, 1946 (Ann Arbor, Mich.: University Microfilms, No. 3214).

6. Ibid., pp. 58, 66.

7. W. E. B. Du Bois, *The Philadelphia Negro* (New York: Schocken Books, 1899; Reprint, Milwood, N.Y.: Kraus International Publications, 1973).

8. W. E. B. Du Bois, *The Health and Physique of the Negro American* (Atlanta, Ga.: Atlanta University Press, 1906).

9. Herbert M. Morais, *The History of the Afro-American in Medicine* (Washington, D.C.: Association for the Study of Negro Life and History, 1978), p. 86.

10. Ibid.

11. Quoted in Roi Ottley, *The Lonely Warrior: The Life and Times of Robert S. Abbott* (Chicago: Henry Regnery, 1955), p. 164.

12. Elmer P. Martin and Joanne M. Martin, *The Black Extended Family* (Chicago: University of Chicago Press, 1978), p. 83.

13. E. Franklin Frazier, *The Negro Family in the United States* (Chicago: University of Chicago Press, 1969), p. 229.

14. Martin and Martin, *The Black Extended Family.*

15. William H. Grier and Price M. Cobbs, *Black Rage* (New York: Basic Books, 1968), p. 103.

16. See *The Holy Qu-ran,* Abdullah Yusuf Ali, trans. (Washington, D.C.: McGregor & Werner, 1946), Vol. 1, p. 39.

17. See T. W. Adorno et al., *The Authoritarian Personality* (New York: Harper & Row, 1950).

18. See E. Franklin Frazier, *Black Bourgeoisie* (New York: Macmillan Co., 1961).

19. See Lee Rainwater, "Crucible of Identity: The Negro Lower-Class Family," *Daedalus,* 95 (Winter 1966), pp. 172, 216.

20. Ibid., p. 206.

21. David Shultz, *Growing Up Black* (Englewood Cliffs, N.J.: Prentice-Hall, 1969), p. 82.

22. Ibid., p. 85.

23. Ibid., p. 82.

24. Ibid., p. 177.

25. Ibid., p. 34.

26. Charles Kiel, *Urban Blues* (Chicago: University of Chicago Press, 1966), pp. 16, 17.

27. Ibid.

28. Ibid., p. 15.

29. Ulf Hannerz, *Soulside* (New York: Columbia University Press, 1969), p. 177.

30. Ibid., p. 153.

31. See Thomas Kochman, ed., *Rappin' and Stylin' Out* (Urbana: University of Illinois Press, 1972).

32. See Lee Rainwater, ed., *Soul* (Chicago: Aldine Publishing Co., 1970).

5 THE BLACK HELPING TRADITION AND SOCIAL WORK

In traditional Africa, natural helping networks promoted the welfare of the people, and the slaves carried over these natural helping networks from Africa to this country. One example of this carry over were the black midwives who delivered most of the babies on slave plantations. The black midwives had learned about delivering babies and sex hygiene in traditional Africa, had brought their knowledge with them, and passed it on. For instance, they used snake oil for healing "the post-birth wounds of the mother," for curing infections, and for "cleaning" purposes—a practice they had learned in Africa.[1] Another tradition that was brought from Africa was the use of "sugar tits" to nourish black babies while their mothers worked in the fields. A sugar tit was a clean rag that was rolled up and "filled with grapevine water and honey."[2] Black babies nursed these "sugar tits until they went to sleep."[3]

Black midwives delivered both black babies and white babies. As Diggs, a Maryland historian and scholar on midwifery, wrote: "Black midwives delivered about 80 percent of the babies born in the western section of Charles County from the early days to 1924."[4] These midwives also taught sex hygiene to black women and white women and even performed abortions. Black midwives were prevalent throughout this country; they were important because physicians in rural areas were scarce and, as Diggs stated, "knew little, if anything, more than the experienced midwives."[5] Black midwifery survived way into the twentieth century, until physicians found delivering babies to be a lucrative market and had black midwives practically legislated out of existence.

Free blacks during slavery created formal social welfare institutions that functioned alongside the natural helping networks to combat the poverty and misery of the free blacks and to seek the freedom of the slaves. Taking a generalist approach, these formal institutions attempted to deal with a wide range of social problems and needs. For example, a benevolent society was likely to be concerned with helping the indigent, taking care of orphans, serving the aged, providing burial funds, and educating the illiterate, as well as seeking the abolition of slavery.

When slavery ended, Rabinowitz wrote, "the growing number of antebellum local institutions such as orphanages, hospitals, and almhouses or state facilities such as insane asylums and institutions for the blind, deaf, and dumb were limited, with few exceptions, to whites."[6] By 1890, state and local governments had created social welfare institutions for blacks on a separate but equal basis.[7] But in terms of funding, facilities, and overall commitment, these segregated almhouses, insane asylums, and so forth were anything but equal and required the nickle-and-dime donations from the masses of poor blacks to remain open. Therefore, throughout the Reconstruction period, although blacks received tremendous aid from the Freedmen's Bureau and various missionary societies, they were still largely responsible for shouldering the burden of caring for the needs of black people, just as they were in slavery.

In the early years of the new century, the mass of black people continued to be the primary funders of black helping institutions. For example, a nursing home for the elderly in Raleigh, North Carolina, was kept open by poor working-class blacks who "pledged one pound of food a month and at least twenty five cents per year in cash and more when due necessity."[8] Blacks helping blacks was so strong in the first decade of this century that Booker T. Washington boasted that "the Negro race in America, unlike many freed races, has not proven a burden upon the pocketbooks of the nation."[9] Washington and many other race leaders were convinced that, despite the barriers confronting blacks, blacks were as capable as any other race of providing for themselves. But then came the Great Depression, which had a resounding impact on the black helping tradition.

GREAT DEPRESSION AND THE DECLINE OF CAREGIVING

With the coming of the Great Depression, the black community, as in most crises, responded with all the charitable strength it could muster. Extended families absorbed thousands of homeless, jobless relatives; black churches opened up soup kitchens, gave out clothing, and engaged in other acts of charity. For instance, the cult leader, Father Divine, fed so many people in Harlem that many of his followers, black and white, believed he must have been God himself and wondered where he got so much food to feed so many people each day.[10] However, even with the efforts of extended families, churches, and other traditional black charitable organizations and the performance of "miracles," the Great Depression made the number of blacks helping other blacks decline sharply.

Already economically less well off than almost every other group in society, blacks saw their plight become worse during the Great Depression. After a while, the depression forced even strong extended families to retreat into themselves, to concern themselves primarily with the survival of their members, and to withdraw the focus of their mutual aid from the wider black community. Although thousands of black families across the nation could not have survived the depression without the aid of kin, many black families had trouble feeding themselves, let alone their relatives, and began either to try to become free of the responsibility of helping relatives or to take on a parasitic relationship with them.

As the Great Depression began to take its toll, the practice of taking responsibility for the care of other blacks began to diminish. Poor and working-class blacks, from whom the bulk of black social welfare funds traditionally came, could no longer contribute to care-giving institutions as they had before because they needed every penny they had to keep themselves and their families alive. This meant that institutions which depended on the nickle-and-dime donations of the black masses suffered greatly. One by one, black social welfare institutions began to cease operation as blacks found it difficult to raise the necessary funds to keep them open.

In the meantime, as the Great Depression began to destroy the economic lives and sap the charitable spirit of blacks and whites alike, the government began to take a more active role in social welfare. President Franklin Delano Roosevelt's New Deal programs, established to pull the country out of the depression, were, in many ways, hostile to the interests of the black people. The New Deal's housing policies "gave formal recognition to residential segregation."[11] Its economic policies "gave official sanction to local patterns of discrimination in employment."[12] Its agricultural policy, which allowed farmers to collect money for not planting or plowing crops, caused the unemployment of a number of black work hands. The Tennessee Valley

Authority barred blacks from its construction activities. Despite the sympathies of President Roosevelt and particularly of his wife, Eleanor Roosevelt, for the downtrodden, "the New Deal did nothing to end segregation or to improve Black education, or to open jobs to Blacks, or to restore the vote."[13] Yet blacks were enthusiastic supporters of President Roosevelt. Not since Abraham Lincoln had they shown such political loyalty. As Lacy wrote:

> . . .the Northern urban Negro vote, which was to become more crucial, shifted massively from the Republican to the Democratic party. There were reasons for this. The New Deal aided the poor through work relief programs and welfare grants to which blacks were admitted. Though the administration of these programs tended to favor whites over blacks, poverty was so much worse among Negroes that any acts to ameliorate it were a special boon to the black community.[14]

Extremely grateful for the meager relief they received in the face of the Great Depression, blacks began to look more and more toward the government for survival. And, as Frazier observed, "the mutual aid society, which once provided protection in times of crises, lost meaning in a world where social assistance was provided by great impersonal organizations."[15] Blacks came increasingly to believe that it was primarily the government's responsibility rather than that of their self-help, mutual-aid systems to care for their needy. Although these self-help efforts had been insufficient to meet the massive needs and problems confronting black Americans, they had made blacks feel some sense of obligation for the care of other blacks and had given them a sense of pride.

DESEGREGATION AND ASSIMILATIONISM

When the country was finally on its way to recovery from the Great Depression and with the coming of World War II, there was yet another force that contributed to the decline of the black helping tradition. Ironically, this force was the continuous drive of blacks toward full participation in the overall American society. It was not just a time of oppression and poverty—conditions with which black people had been familiar since their arrival in this country. It was also a radical, fast-moving time of profound social and psychological change. It was a time not for equilibrium but for upheaval, for experimentation as much as for preservation, and for new adaptations to the demands of a world moving faster than it had done before.

Values did not seem as permanent anymore. The chain of continuity, if not broken altogether, was beginning to unbind. The new generation had its own challenges and its problems of finding a way to make a way, and the ways of the elders did not always seem appropriate to meet the urgency of the time. It is no wonder even that the old race men and race women who had forged many of the traditions of earlier generations were being challenged by a new black leadership. As Young described:

> [The depression era] saw the rise to prominence of a new generation of men and women whose orientation toward the problems and culture of black America often departed substantially from that of the older generation. Probably the most important basis for difference between the older and the younger generations resided in the fact that the older men were "race men." Many of these younger writers charged that [these race men] had given Black Americans an excessively provincial view.[16]

The new leadership tended to think that the problems of blacks were really the problems of class, not necessarily those of race. They pressed for assimilation and participation in the dominant society with little regard for the preservation of old race values, which they associated with the old era of segregation.

Under the leadership of such organizations as the National Association for the Advancement of Colored People and such leaders as A. Philip Randolph and Walter White, the civil rights movement took shape again and began to break down barrier after barrier, culminating in the powerful civil rights movement of the mid-1950s and 1960s that nearly tore down the walls of segregation in this country. The assimilationists made gains that helped blacks of all walks of life. These gains made it possible for all blacks to move a bit more easily, freely, and securely. But now that blacks could receive social services from the government like anyone else, what use was there for black orphanages, old-folks' homes, and other black helping institutions? Was not the maintenance of these institutions, born largely out of enforced racial separation and the perpetuation of segregation, an impediment to the aim of blacks for full, equal participation in the society?

URBANIZATION

In Chapter 4, we discussed the impact of urbanization on the helping tradition of black people, but it is appropriate here to make a few remarks as well. As blacks were steadily becoming an urbanized people, the focus of black leaders and black caregiving began to shift from the rural blacks to the urban blacks. Black caregivers were beginning to see that the problems of urban blacks were too massive to be tackled through single helping institutions. The benevolent societies, women's clubs, churches, and fraternal orders of the last century were geared toward solving a host of social ills. However, as blacks confronted the massive problems of big-city life, greater specialization became a feature of the black helping tradition. It was demonstrated by the movement for housing reform, better health care for blacks, better recreational facilities, and so on. Black leaders were coming to believe that the social welfare institutions needed to address the massive problems of urban blacks could not be funded by the masses of poor black people. Therefore, they were more inclined to turn to the various levels of government for legislation and funding directed at solving many of the social problems confronting black people.

Two or three decades after the Great Depression ended, the new generation of blacks were far away from the core values and traditions that had brought blacks along the way. The younger generation did not have to suffer many of the hardships of their elders. They were not living in a time when sharing was vital to survival. They were growing up in an age of rapid desegregation in which few or no orphanages, old folks' homes, schools, or hospitals were run by and for black people. They were growing up at a time when insurance companies had replaced the mutual-aid functions of fraternal orders and benevolent societies and when the government had taken over a large share of the social services provided to black people. In integrated schools, they were being taught to value individualism, rugged competition, and meritocracy, and they were more in tune with the heroes and heroines of the popular culture than with the old "race men" and "race women" who had placed so much emphasis on self-help, education, uplift, and pride. They were more of an urban people than a rural people now, and, hence, were largely influenced by fad-oriented "go for self" ways of big-city life. When they desperately needed help, it was not to the lay caregivers or the natural helping networks in their own communities that they turned, but to trained, professional social workers.

PROFESSIONALIZATION OF BLACK CAREGIVING

With desegregation making all-black charitable institutions less necessary and with the government playing a larger, even dominant, role in social welfare endeavors, blacks became more content to be recipients of aid than dispensers of it. Feeling more and more that their own natural helping networks were unreliable for tackling many of their problems, they came to see black caregiving as less a responsibility for each and every black person and more a responsibility of the emerging trained professional social workers.

However, even with the professionalization of social work, the black tradition continued to play a part. Collins and Pancoast wrote that "Were it not for the informal services of helping networks, social agencies—whether they recognize it or not—would be swamped."[17] Natural helping networks, such as the black extended family, helped cut down the burdensome caseloads of professional social workers. But even more important was the role the black helping tradition played in motivating black people to choose a career in social work. Many, if not most, blacks who were motivated to choose social work as a profession did so because they came from extended families or from a highly religious culture and because being a part of an oppressed, impoverished people, they had personally witnessed the struggles of their race. They chose social work as a career because they believed that, as trained social workers, they would be able to provide higher-quality social services than black people could receive from the largely untrained caregivers of the past. As far back as 1938, Johnson was calling on blacks to become trained social workers so they could help alleviate the massive problems and unmet needs of black people:

> The census for 1930 lists 211 male and 827 female Negro social and welfare workers. This total of 1,038 gives a ratio of one social worker to every 11,456 Negroes. The ratio suggests the need for larger numbers in this field. With the large number of Negroes on the relief rolls of the country and the need for more constant and increased recreational and welfare activities generally there is a likelihood that demand will continue for well-educated social workers.[18]

The demand continued, and blacks took up the call. Today, the concentration of blacks in social work is as heavy as it was in the teaching and preaching professions of the past. In a sense, professional black social workers have become new to the black legacy of helping. But almost from the beginning of the entry of blacks into the profession, there were conflicts. In the beginning of the twentieth century, the budding social work profession had taken on much of the moralistic and individualistic, Social Darwinistic baggage of the late nineteenth century. Social workers or charity workers often tied issues such as poverty to the morality and character defects of individuals. And, generally, it was thought that blacks basically were an immoral, lazy, unambitious people—the least fit for survival and participation in society. The cure, of course, for the ills blacks faced was to bolster up their moral fiber with heavy doses of the Christian spirit and the values of Calvinism and rugged individualism.

Social work further conflicted with the black helping tradition when it began to move away from the environmentalist perspective, taken on largely by settlement houses and other community organizations, and assumed a psychoanalytic emphasis. It was not that blacks had been left without serious psychological scars from centuries of racism. Self-hatred, identification with the oppressor, and the general rage, bitterness, frustrations, and depression that came with being constantly mistreated and abused were indelible marks on the psyche of black people. Black leaders spent a great deal of time trying to keep up the hopes of black people so they would not succumb to alienation, apathy, and despair. And probably, psychoanalytically oriented social workers would have been better prepared to deal with many of the mental problems of black people than the natural helping networks that had little understanding of mental health needs. However, the conflict came because social work's heavy emphasis on Freudian analysis deemphasized the massive social problems of poverty, ignorance, racism, and disease to which black care-giving systems and black caregivers generally addressed themselves.

Underlying Conflicts with Social Work

The underlying basic conflict that black social workers were having with their profession was racism. One chief issue that received a great deal of attention was the extent to which black social workers should work with white clients and white social workers should work with black clients. But the conflict was much larger than this issue. A basic problem was that social work relied heavily on the social science literature, particularly that of psychology and sociology. Much of this literature viewed black people in a deviant, negative perspective and the black family in a pathology-disorganization perspective.[19] This perspective often focused heavily on deficits in the black family; perceived it to be a matrifocal, maladaptive institution; and suggested that it should be like the patriarchal, nuclear family of the white middle class. This attitude caused social workers, educators, and practitioners to ignore the role of the extended family and other elements of the black culture in the survival of black people and made them see blacks basically as a deviant, dependent people who must be made healthy with the endowment of white middle-class values. It also left black social workers to assume a liberal, mainstream, white middle-class reformist perspective of social work.

It was largely as a result of the black-consciousness mood of the 1960s that black social workers began to demand that social work view black social welfare from more of a black perspective. Black social workers became increasingly discontent with the paternalistic ways that black people were being viewed in social work and by the profession's image of blacks as deviants—pathological people with no history, no culture, and no pride.

During the 1960s, black social workers wanted the profession to know about the contribution of blacks to social welfare and the efforts of blacks to help themselves. They were aware that there have always been blacks who were too status conscious, too color conscious (feeling that blacks with lighter skin are superior to blacks with darker skin), and too individualistic to concern themselves with the masses of black people. They also were well aware that there were slaves who looked down on other slaves; free blacks who treated slaves in a condescending, paternalistic manner that sometimes was displayed in outright contempt; and some blacks who built schools, churches, and fraternal orders not because they cared about the welfare of black people but because they wanted to maintain exclusiveness or to keep a social distance between them and those they considered beneath them. But many of these black social workers were equally aware that black people have never been the irresponsible, helpless, dependent people they were so often depicted to be in the social science literature. They knew that helping has been an intimate and profound factor in the life and history of black people.

Important Questions

Because social work touches the broken lives of black people to such a great extent, these race-conscious black social workers of the 1960s believed that a focus on the strength, resources, and support systems of black people might prove more fruitful to social workers than would the concentration on pathologies, deviance, and deficits that was the preoccupation of much of the social work that was borrowed from the social sciences. Not denying that black people suffer pathologies, too, these social workers seemed to be suggesting that when assessing the resources necessary to solve problems pertaining to the black individual and the black family, it might be helpful to raise such questions as these:

■ How strong are family ties, and to what extent do family members come to the aid of one another?

■ What is the relationship of well-off family members and less well-off ones, and to what extent do lower-class and middle-class family members aid one another?

■ How strong are male-female relationships, and to what extent do black men and black women work together on a basis of equality for the survival and advancement of one another and the overall family?

■ How close are family members to the children, and to what extent are prosocial values instilled in children?

■ How strong is the religious or spiritual life of the individuals or family members, and to what extent do they rely on spiritual resources for greater stability in their personal lives and in the family and for reaching out to aid other people in the black community and the wider society?

■ How race conscious are family members, and to what extent is racial consciousness a source of inspiration, pride, therapy, and commitment to black liberation and social change?

■ Which institutions, agencies, or natural helping networks are in the black community and the wider society to help black people survive, advance, and realize their human potential and promise?

These questions are rooted in the black culture and tradition. They prescribe how blacks have traditionally or historically behaved in the context of their daily lives. And they suggest that black people can deviate not only from the norms of the dominant society but from the norms of black culture. Thus, when a street black cons another black, he can be said to be deviating from the black culture because, although there have been black conmen in every period, blacks traditionally have frowned on this behavior and definitely have not wanted to pass down this behavior through the generations. In the same sense, black men may want to dominate black women or blacks may feel a sense of alienation and despair. But the black tradition emphasizes male-female equality and the maintenance of faith and hope in one's abilities to overcome. Generally, questions of this nature do not suggest that black social workers cannot learn from the social work literature that does not have a black perspective. These questions merely suggest that a black perspective exists and that it should be considered by social workers.

The Profession's Response

The general cry of black social workers was for a black perspective on social work. In a sense, they were calling on social workers to develop a positive racial or ethnic consciousness and to broaden their concept of social justice by analyzing and attacking racist social systems. Many black social workers formed the National Association of Black Social Workers and other black social welfare organizations to issue their challenge to the profession. The major social work organizations, such as the Council on Social Work Education and the National Association of Social Workers, responded by promoting the need to incorporate ethnic-related content into social work education and practice. As Solomon wrote, the profession generally responded by including "new content and courses on racism and minority groups," by holding numerous "workshops, colloquia, and seminars for agency personnel to sensitize staff to minority lifestyles and value systems" and by increasing "efforts to recruit black and other minority students into graduate schools of social work."[20]

The black-consciousness mood in the black community prevailed throughout the turbulent 1960s. However, by the mid-1970s, that mood was steadily losing ground. The main reason for the decline in racial consciousness was that there were no black institutions to sustain it. In other words, when it did not become structured in black families, black churches, schools, and the media, black consciousness lost its force and vitality. Institutionalization means that the black tradition does not depend solely on charismatic leaders, popularity, or the mood of the times to perpetuate it from generation to generation. It also means that the tradition receives greater legitimacy. Because the black-consciousness mood was not institutionalized, it was difficult to retain, particularly when it was contending with other powerful forces in the society, such as the bourgeoisie and street ideologies. To a large extent, the social work profession was able to do what many highly race-conscious blacks were unable to do: To institutionalize the black-consciousness mood of the 1960s at a time when it had failed to be institutionalized in other areas affecting black life.

THE FUTURE OF BLACK SOCIAL WORKERS

Social workers of all races are faced with a similar problem in this country: they are working in a profession that receives low priority in the overall American society. Individualism and profit making as the dominant motivating forces in this society may actually be incompatible with human welfare. To be sure, this country has done much to perpetuate three major ills that social workers are committed to correcting: poverty, racism, and sexism. To a great extent, there are parallels to the ways black people and the social work profession are treated in this society. Blacks are relegated to an inferior status, as is social work as a profession. Like blacks, social work greatly depends on funds from the government for survival, and the condition of both blacks and the profession worsens or improves according to fluctuations in the economy or the political interest shown them at the moment. Moreover, both blacks and social work are subjected to the hostility of right-wing groups, which makes it conceivable that if some right-wing extremists had their way, black people and social workers, so-called bleeding hearts, would suffer a terrible fate. But even though the profession, again like blacks, is sorely circumscribed in what it can do to effectuate the social changes it desires, it can be predicted that black social workers will not only urge the profession to continue and to enhance its institutionalization of the black perspective but will seek to get social workers to exert greater pressure on the society for social change.

Although slavery ended over a hundred years ago, the lives of the majority of black people are still wretched. Every year, the National Urban League issues a report on the "state of black America," and each year the report presents a depressing picture of black life, politically, socially, and economically. Herman J. Blake, a sociologist, reported that if one analyzed the rates at which blacks were gaining economic and educational parity with whites and then extrapolated these rates to determine how long it would take for actual parity, one would find that "at the 1950–60 rates of change, it would take 60 years in education, 93 years in occupation, 219 years in income of persons, and 805 years in family income."[21] It must be noted that the 1960s were a time of rapid social change for blacks and that the process has slowed down considerably since then. This decline in the rate of change is one basis for the authors' prediction that, in the next few years, black social workers will exert greater pressure on the power structure for change.

Another basis for the authors' prediction is that many black social workers have realized or will come to realize that no matter how well blacks have cooperated in helping one another, black self-help efforts or black caregiving have never been sufficient to move a large number of blacks from poverty, despair, and stunted lives. The problems that black people have faced throughout their stay in this country have not been insurmountable, but they have been too massive for black people to tackle alone. Then, also, blacks did not create the problems alone, as the history of their continuous victimization confirms. It always has been necessary for the government to deal with the massive social problems of a people who have been denied, generation after generation, the fruits of social, political, and economic democracy. So far, the government has responded in a piecemeal, conservative, often oppressive and stigmatizing, fashion—one that has been insufficient to keep generation after generation of black Americans from suffering extreme hardship and deprivation. Thus, if black social workers are to help their people, they will have to work with other social workers in continuing or renewing their commitment to social welfare; stepping up their struggle to combat poverty, sexism, and racism; and exerting greater pressure on those forces that undermine the welfare of black people and thwart the goal of real political, economic, and social democracy for all American citizens.

In envisioning the probable course that black social workers will take in the future, the authors further predict that black social workers will urge the profession to expand its focus beyond the United States. As black social workers become increasingly conscious of the plight of blacks throughout the world, coming face to face with such stark realities as the daily death of thousands of Africans by starvation, they will strive for the greater globalization of social work. That is, American black social workers will play a major role in forming an international network of social workers from all over the world to deal more urgently than ever before with such worldwide problems as hunger, housing, health, and education.

The more that black social workers concern themselves with racism, the more they will find that it is a worldwide phenomenon and that domestic racism has international linkages. Furthermore, as black social workers broaden their perspective on such problems as poverty, sexism, and class exploitation, they will take a more active interest in the welfare not just of black people, here and abroad, but of all people—brown, yellow, red, and white. Then, as heirs of the black care-giving legacy, they will help extend the communal spirit from the extended family to the nation and from the nation to the whole society of humankind.

REFERENCES

1. William A. Diggs, "Midwifery in Charles County, Maryland," *The Maryland Pendulum* (Annapolis: Maryland Commission on Afro-American History and Culture, Spring 1983), Vol. 3, p. 6.
2. Ibid.
3. Ibid.
4. Ibid., p. 3.
5. Ibid.

6. Howard N. Rabinowitz, "From Exclusion to Segregation: Health and Welfare Services for Southern Blacks, 1865–1890," *Social Service Review,* 48 (September 1974), p. 327.

7. Ibid., p. 328.

8. William L. Pollard, *A Study in Black Self-Help* (San Francisco: R & E Associates, 1978), p. 113.

9. Quoted in ibid., p. 97.

10. See John Hosner, *God in a Rolls Royce* (Freeport, N.Y.: Books for Libraries Press, 1971).

11. Dan Lacy, *The White Use of Blacks in America* (New York: McGraw-Hill Book Co., 1972).

12. Ibid., pp. 54–55.

13. Ibid., p. 168.

14. Ibid.

15. E. Franklin Frazier, *Black Bourgeoisie* (New York: Macmillan Co., 1961), p. 103.

16. James O. Young, *Black Writers of the Thirties* (Baton Rouge: Louisiana State University Press, 1973), pp. xi.

17. Alice H. Collins and Diane L. Pancoast, *Natural Helping Networks* (Washington, D.C.: National Association of Social Workers, 1976), p. 25.

18. Charles S. Johnson, *The Negro College Graduate* (Chapel Hill: University of North Carolina Press, 1938), pp. 268–269.

19. Elmer P. Martin and Joanne M. Martin, *The Black Extended Family* (University of Chicago Press, 1978), p. 104.

20. Barbara Bryant Solomon, *Black Empowerment: Social Work in Oppressed Communities* (New York: Columbia University Press, 1976), pp. 79–80.

21. Quoted in Andrew Billingsley, *Black Families in White America* (Englewood Cliffs, N.J.: Prentice-Hall, 1968), p. 168.

6 SUMMARY

Although social scientists have taken it for granted that black Americans have no traditions, black traditions in religion, protest, music, uplift, and other areas have been evident throughout black American history. Another strong tradition has been the helping tradition. This book has attempted not so much to document the existence of the black helping tradition as to present a theory of the tradition's origin, development, and decline. In this sense, the book has rested more on analysis than description. Its intent was to give people in the helping professions, particularly social workers, a better understanding of this important tradition that cuts across crucial areas of black life and culture.

The theory presented here is that the black helping tradition has its origin or roots in the black extended family, particularly the extended family's emphasis on cooperation between men and women and among people of different social classes or status groups, the prosocialization of children, and mutual aid. The tradition was extended from the family through fictive kinship, religious consciousness, and racial consciousness to touch nearly every facet of life in the black community.

Historically, blacks always had a strong helping tradition. In traditional Africa, the concept of mutual aid permeated the entire philosophy and life of the community. The extended family was the foundation for the helping tradition. Although the African family was patriarchal to a large extent and though goods were not always distributed evenly, no individual was allowed to go hungry or without shelter while others hoarded food or had shelter to spare. Even the most powerful patriarch could not put his self-interest above the general welfare of the group.

So strong was the helping tradition in Africa that it survived the devastating impact of the slave trade and was carried by the slaves to this country. In this country, it functioned more in a noninstitutional than an institutional form, and, of course, freed from its original cultural moorings, it took on new shape and meaning. Here the tradition survived largely in the hearts and souls of the transplanted Africans and was reinforced by a variety of forces, including the efforts to survive slavery, black leaders, new arrivals from Africa, and the memories of the slaves who reminisced about life in their African homeland.

Slavery provided a great impetus for blacks to come together around one of their strongest cultural traits: helping one another. Although it severely weakened the patriarchy of the traditional African society, ironically, the downfall of black patriarchy made for the crude equalization of black women and black men, who had little choice but to work together to survive. Contrary to what many scholars allege, matriarchy had little chance of developing in slavery. Indeed, a strong case has been made that black women were special captives because they not only had to bear the burdens that black men had to bear, but they had to serve as breeders and sex objects.

The extended slave family involved more than just blood relatives and relatives by "marriage." Slaves adopted relatives and established a fictive kinship network that encompassed the entire slave community. Fictive kinship enlarged social obligations and extended the slaves' mutual-aid efforts for survival. The mutual-aid efforts were particularly evident in the care of older slaves, the rearing of children, and even the religious and budding racial consciousness of the slaves. Religious consciousness served as a kind of therapy for the wounded psyche and soul of the slaves. The belief that God was on their side gave them a sense of spiritual advantage over the slave master. The undeveloped racial consciousness among the slaves was demonstrated most markedly by acts of protest and rebelliousness, both overt and covert.

The fictive kinship ties allowed for the emergence of status-group cooperation among the broadest status groups on the plantation: the house slaves, the field slaves, and the skilled slaves. Contrary to popular thinking, the slaves cooperated with one another in numerous ways that were crucial to their survival. That the house slaves and skilled slaves had relatives and friends who were field slaves made it easier for them to feel they all were subject to a similar fate.

Free blacks also cooperated significantly with their slave brothers and sisters. Although heavily oppressed and living in a state of semislavery themselves, they made many sacrifices and took many risks to help the slaves escape from bondage. The fictive kinship that was the primary device for enlarging social relationships among slaves grew into a more developed form of racial unity or racial consciousness. This sense of racial consciousness produced "race men" and "race women" whose entire being was oriented to the protection, survival, advancement, and redemption of the black race.

Racial consciousness led to the institutionalization of the black helping tradition, as free blacks built elaborate networks of caring, sharing, and helping through their churches, fraternal orders, and schools. The extended family and the black church were the two most powerful care-giving institutions. Schools, temperance societies, and organized protest groups also played an important role in the uplift of blacks. Free blacks saw schools as the instrument for overcoming the need to do menial labor—work that had become associated with blacks and was dubbed "nigger work." Race men and race women strongly advocated temperance not only because they saw it as a necessary element of black uplift but because they did not want black people to be stereotyped as a race of drunkards. Protest by the free blacks was aimed at the Fugitive Slave Law and "man-stealing," as well as at obtaining rights for black people.

In the institutionalization of the black helping tradition, women as well as men played deciding roles. Race-conscious men and women strongly believed that their race could not rise above the condition of its women. Hence, they fought patriarchy on every level because they considered women to be the indispensable economic and political partners of men.

Patriarchy had always been a threat to the black helping tradition. For here, in contrast to traditional Africa, patriarchy was not checked by customs and subordinated to the welfare of the group. In its demand that women play subordinate roles to men and that men separate themselves from their unfortunate brothers, patriarchy made for class divisiveness and the repression of the talents of women. It threatened to break down the extended family and fictive kinship ties as well as the racial consciousness necessary for the development and growth of care-giving institutions.

The Civil War and gradual emancipation left many black people ragged, hungry, diseased, and shelterless. Blacks were free, but they had none of the conditions for survival and protection. Patriarchy became more widespread as black men sought their "rightful" place as heads of the family and as authority figures in black institutions. Patriarchy became particularly dominant in a leading black care-giving institution—the black church. Despite the rise of patriarchy, the practice of mutual aid and caregiving was unprecedented as blacks sought to reconstruct lives broken by war and devastated by years of bondage.

Never before had the masses of poor, ignorant, broken black people been so enthusiastic about uplifting themselves. Hence, funds for care-giving efforts came largely from their nickle-and-dime donations. These funds were used to build homes for the aged and for orphans and to provide for other poor, needy blacks. Furthermore, even with the growing patriarchy, black women continued to play a vital role in the care and uplift of their people through women's clubs, which became a predominant type of black charitable organization. Even with the unprecedented struggles of blacks to rise above the shadow of the plantation, reconstruction of black life was a failure for the most part because their condition required much more massive caregiving than the enthusiastic and noble efforts made by blacks to help themselves.

The turn of the twentieth century saw the continuation of the black care-giving heritage amid segregation, racial consciousness, and religious consciousness. However, it also saw the decline of this tradition, particularly with the Great Depression of the 1930s and the consequent end of black charitable endeavors because the nickles and dimes from the masses of blacks were now desperately needed for the survival of the family and of the individual. The Great Depression brought about greater governmental intervention in social welfare. This intervention contributed to the decline in black caregiving in that blacks came to depend heavily on governmental aid that was dispensed largely by professional care-giving agents and that was particularly welcomed because the Great Depression was making a shambles of black care-giving institutions. Ironically, desegregation and the movement toward assimilation provided the impetus for blacks to strive more and more to participate in the care-giving systems of the wider society. In the rigid segregated world, blacks had little choice but to close ranks around their own care-giving institutions if they were to be cared for at all. But as the wider society became more liberal in its social services to blacks, black people responded accordingly.

The black care-giving tradition was strong in both rural and urban areas. In all-black communities, it was even stronger than in biracial communities because the people were freed from most of the pressures of racial tension. Even the migration of blacks from rural to urban areas found the helping tradition in operation when members of extended families migrated to the cities and paved the way for others. Moreover, people from small towns who came to the urban areas tended to live in close proximity to kin and friends and thus tended to form ties with others from their hometown.

In earlier periods, black caregiving was just as powerful in the cities as it was in rural and small-town areas, and life in the big cities demanded even more new efforts at black caregiving. However, even though the extended family is still a strong institution in urban areas today and even with scattered, isolated acts of blacks helping blacks in institutions such as the black church, the urban community, with its emphasis on competition, individualism, and money making has seen a rapid decline in the black helping tradition.

Two urban-oriented ideologies—the bourgeoisie ideology and the street ideology—have particularly hurt the black helping tradition. The bourgeoisie ideology, although it stresses hard work, success, education, moral discipline, and individual initiative, emphasizes individualism, which has led blacks to think they are not as responsible for the welfare of other blacks as they were in the past. The street ideology, which stresses conning, manipulation, and exploitation, has been most damaging to the black helping tradition. Yet, ironically, it is this deviant, criminal ideology that many social scientists see as the authentic black culture.

In the past, the black helping tradition was strong when the major elements of the extended family were strong and when fictive kinship, racial consciousness, and religious consciousness were powerful enough to carry the helping tradition in the family to such major institutions in the black community as churches, schools, and women's clubs. But today, although the extended family is still a powerful mechanism for the survival of black people in both rural and urban areas, its major elements have grown weak. Its elements of mutual aid and social-class cooperation are plagued by the bourgeoisie and street ideologies and a reliance by blacks on governmental aid. Male-female cooperation has declined, as indicated by increasing divorce, separation, and desertion rates among blacks and a sharp rise in single-parent households. And the prosocialization of children is made more difficult because even when blacks teach their children prosocial values at home, these values are not reinforced in the school system and in the wider society.

The decline of racial consciousness in blacks has made it especially difficult to transfer helping, caring, and sharing values to the black community. Racial consciousness has been strong at critical moments in history; even today, blacks are still struggling to raise the racial consciousness of other black people. But the failure to institu-

Summary   **95**

tionalize black consciousness has made it difficult to keep the mood strong from one generation to the next. This problem was nowhere more evident than after the 1960s. Racial consciousness was probably stronger during the 1960s than in any other decade in black American history. However, by the mid-1970s, it was all but dead—largely because it had not been institutionalized.

In traditional Africa and in slavery, natural helping networks such as the extended family promoted the welfare of the people. Free blacks were able to institutionalize black caregiving. The black helping institutions took a generalist approach and tried to solve a wide range of problems confronting black people. After the emancipation of the slaves, so-called separate-but-equal social services were created by some state and local governments, but because of the poor quality of these services, blacks still had to rely heavily on their own initiatives.

Black caregiving was still strong in the first two decades of this century; then came the depression, followed by massive governmental intervention. Soon the professional social worker was the primary helping agent in the black community. As blacks entered the social work profession, they immediately came into conflict with the general negative perspective of and paternalistic approach to black people. The black consciousness mood of the 1960s led black social workers to challenge social work educators and practitioners to see social work from a black perspective. Social workers responded to this challenge by institutionalizing the black perspective in the profession. It is predicted that, in the future, black social workers will seek to get the social work profession to exert greater pressures on the power structure (1) as a means of addressing the extreme poverty and racism that still plague black people over 100 years after emancipation and (2) as a step toward creating a society that gives as much value to human welfare as it does to the making of money and to maintaining the power of a privileged class. It is further predicted that as blacks become more conscious of the plight of black people and other people worldwide, they will take a more international view of social work and, therefore, offer the black helping tradition not just to black people but to all the people of the world.

BIBLIOGRAPHY

Adorno, T. W., et al. *The Authoritarian Personality.* New York: Harper & Row, 1950.

Berlin, Ira. *Slaves without Masters.* New York: Pantheon Books, 1974.

Bernard, Jessie. *Marriage and Family Among Negroes.* Englewood Cliffs, N.J.: Prentice-Hall, 1966.

Billingsley, Andrew. *Black Families in White America.* Englewood Cliffs, N.J.: Prentice-Hall, 1968.

Blassingame, John W. *The Slave Community.* New York: Oxford University Press, 1972.

————. *Slave Testimony.* Baton Rouge: Louisiana State University Press, 1977.

Blyden, Edward Wilmot. *African Life and Customs.* London, England: C. M. Phillips, 1908.

Cheek, William F. *Black Resistance Before the Civil War.* Beverly Hills, Calif.: Glencoe Press, 1970.

Collins, Alice H., and Pancoast, Diane L. *Natural Helping Networks.* Washington, D.C.: National Association of Social Workers, 1976.

Cones, James H. *Black Theology and Black Power.* New York: Seabury Press, 1969.

Conrad, Earl. *Harriet Tubman.* Washington, D.C.: Associated Publishers, 1943.

Cooper, Frederick. "Elevating the Race: The Social Thought of Black Leaders, 1827–1850," *American Quarterly,* 24 (December 1972), pp. 604–625.

Cox, Oliver C. *Caste, Class, and Race.* New York: Doubleday & Co., 1948.

————. *Race Relations.* Detroit: Wayne State University Press, 1976.

Davis, Angela. *Women, Race, and Class.* New York: Random House, 1981.

Delaney, Martin. *The Condition, Elevation, Images and Destiny of the Colored People of the United States of America Politically Considered.* 1852. Reprint. New York: Arno Press, 1969.

Diggs, William A. "Midwifery in Charles County, Maryland," *The Maryland Pendulum.* Annapolis: Maryland Commission on Afro-American History and Culture, Spring 1983, Vol. 3, p. 6.

Douglass, Frederick. *The Life and Times of Frederick Douglass.* 1881. Reprint. New York: Collier Books, 1962.

Drake, St. Clair, and Cayton, Horace. *Black Metropolis.* New York: Harcourt, Brace & World, 1945.

DuBois, W. E. B. *Black Reconstruction in America: 1860–1880.* New York: Russell & Russell, 1935.

———. *Efforts for Social Betterment Among Negro Americans.* Atlanta, Ga.: Atlanta University Press, 1909.

———. *Gift of Black Folk: The Negroes in the Making of America.* 1924. Reprint. New York: AMS Press, 1972.

———. *The Health and Physique of the Negro.* Atlanta, Ga.: Atlanta University Press, 1906.

———. *The Philadelphia Negro.* New York: Schocken Books, 1899. Reprint. Milwood, N.Y.: Kraus International Publications, 1973.

———. *Souls of Black Folk: Essays and Sketches.* 1903. Reprint. Milwood, N.Y.: Kraus International Publications, 1973.

Ellison, Ralph. *Shadow and Act.* New York: Random House, 1964.

Frazier, E. Franklin. *Black Bourgeoisie.* New York: Macmillan Co., 1961.

———. *The Negro Church in America.* Reprint. New York: Schocken Books, 1963.

———. *The Negro Family in the United States.* Chicago: University of Chicago Press, 1969.

———. "Traditions and Patterns of Negro Family Life in the United States," in E. B. Reuter, ed., *Race and Culture Contacts.* New York: McGraw-Hill Book Co., 1934.

Genovese, Eugene D. *Roll, Jordon, Roll.* New York: Pantheon Books, 1974.

Glazer, Nathan, and Moynihan, Daniel P. *Beyond the Melting Pot.* Cambridge, Mass.: M.I.T. Press, 1963.

Grier, William H., and Cobbs, Price M. *Black Rage.* New York: Basic Books, 1968.

Gutman, Herbert G. *The Black Family in Slavery and Freedom, 1750–1925.* New York: Pantheon Books, 1976.

Handlin, Oscar. *The Newcomers.* Cambridge, Mass.: Harvard University Press, 1959.

Hannerz, Ulf. *Soulside.* New York: Columbia University Press, 1969.

Haynes, George Edmund. *The Trend of the Races.* Miami, Fla.: Minemosyne Publishing Co., 1976.

Herskovits, Melville J. *Myth of the Negro Past.* Boston: Beacon Hill Press, 1958.

Hill, Mozell. "The All-Negro Society in Oklahoma." Unpublished doctoral thesis, University of Chicago, 1946. Ann Arbor, Mich.: University Microfilms, No. 3214.

Hobhouse, Leonard T. *Social Evolution and Political Theory.* New York: Columbia University Press, 1911.

Hodge, Merle. "The Shadow of the Whip: A Comment on Male-Female Relations in the Caribbean," in Orde Coombs, ed., *Is Massa Day Dead?* New York: Doubleday & Co., 1971, pp. 111–118.

Holy Bible, Good News Bible: The Bible in Today's English Version. New York: American Bible Society, 1976.

Holy Qu-ran. Abdullah Yusuf Ali (trans.). Washington, D.C.: McGregor & Werner, 1946.

Hosner, John. *God in a Rolls Royce.* Freeport, N.Y.: Books for Libraries Press, 1971.

Hull, Richard W. *Munyakare: African Civilization Before the Batuuree.* New York: John Wiley & Sons, 1972.

Johnson, Charles S. *Shadow of the Plantation.* Chicago: University of Chicago Press, 1934.

————. *The Negro College Graduate.* Chapel Hill: University of North Carolina Press, 1938.

Johnston, Brenda. *Between the Devil and the Sea.* New York: Harcourt Brace Jovanovich, 1974.

Kaplan, Sidney. *The Black Presence in the Era of the American Revolution, 1770–1800.* Washington, D.C.: Smithsonian Press, 1973.

Kardiner, Abram, and Ovesey, Lionel. *The Mark of Oppression.* New York: W. W. Norton & Co., 1951.

Kenyatta, Jomo. *Facing Mt. Kenya.* New York: Vintage Books, 1965.

Kiel, Charles. *Urban Blues.* Chicago: University of Chicago Press, 1966.

Kochman, Thomas (ed.). *Rappin' and Stylin' Out.* Urbana: University of Illinois Press, 1972.

Lacy, Dan. *The White Use of Blacks in America.* New York: McGraw-Hill Book Co., 1972.

Lewis, Hylan. *Blackways of Kent.* Chapel Hill: University of North Carolina Press, 1955.

Lindsay, Inabel B. "The Participation of Negroes in the Establishment of Welfare Services, 1865–1900." Unpublished doctoral thesis, University of Pittsburgh School of Social Work, 1952.

Litwack, Leon F. *Been in the Storm So Long.* New York: Alfred A. Knopf, 1979.

————. *North of Slavery.* Chicago: University of Chicago Press, 1961.

Loewenberg, Bert James, and Bogin, Ruth. *Black Women in Nineteenth-Century American Life.* University Park: Pennsylvania State University Press, 1976.

Lovell, John, Jr. *Black Song: The Forge and the Flame.* New York: Macmillan Co., 1972.

Magdol, Edward. *A Right to the Land: Essays on the Freedmen's Community.* Westport, Conn.: Greenwood Press, 1977.

Martin, Elmer P., and Martin, Joanne M. *The Black Extended Family.* Chicago: University of Chicago Press, 1978.

————. "The Black Woman: Cultural and Economic Captive," in Pauline Kolenda, ed., *Contemporary Cultures For and Against Women.* Houston, Tex.: University of Houston Press, 1981, pp. 235–250.

Mbiti, John S. *African Religion and Philosophy.* New York: Doubleday & Co., 1970.

Millet, Kate. *Sexual Politics.* Garden City, N.Y.: Doubleday & Co., 1970.

Morais, Herbert M. *The History of the Afro-American in Medicine.* Washington, D.C.: Association for the Study of Negro Life and History, 1978.

Moynihan, Daniel Patrick. *The Negro Family: A Case for National Action.* Washington, D.C.: U.S. Department of Labor, Office of Policy, Planning & Research, March 1965.

Myrdal, Gunnar. *An American Dilemma.* New York: Harper & Bros., 1944.

Nyerere, Julius. *Freedom and Socialism.* New York: Oxford University Press, 1968.

————. *Freedom and Unity.* London, England: Oxford University Press, 1966.

Odum, Howard. *Social and Mental Traits of the Negro.* New York: AMS Press, 1910.

Ottley, Roi. *The Lonely Warrior: The Life and Times of Robert S. Abbott.* Chicago: Henry Regnery, 1955.

Owens, Leslie Howard. *This Species of Property.* New York: Oxford University Press, 1976.

Painter, Nell. *The Exodusters.* New York: Alfred A. Knopf, 1977.

Park, Mungo. *Travels in Africa.* New York: M. McFarlane, 1901.

Patterson, Orlando. "Toward a Future that Has No Past—Reflections on the Fate of Blacks in the Americas," *Public Interest,* 27 (Spring 1972), pp. 25–62.

Pease, Jane H., and Pease, William H. *They Who Would Be Free.* New York: Atheneum Publishers, 1974.

Pollard, William L. *A Study in Black Self-Help.* San Francisco: R & E Associates, 1978.

Powdermaker, Hortense. *After Freedom.* New York: Viking Press, 1939.

Quarles, Benjamin. *Black Abolitionists.* New York: Oxford University Press, 1969.

————. *The Negro in the Making of America*. New York: Collier Books, 1964.

Rabinowitz, Howard N. "From Exclusion to Segregation: Health and Welfare Services for Southern Blacks, 1865–1890," *Social Service Review*, 48 (September 1974), pp. 327–354.

Rainwater, Lee. "Crucible of Identity: The Negro Lower-Class Family," *Daedalus*, 95 (Winter 1966), pp. 172–216.

————(ed.). *Soul*. Chicago: Aldine Publishing Co., 1970.

Rogers, J. A. *World's Great Men of Color*. Vol. 2. New York: Collier Books, 1972.

Ross, Edyth. *The Black Heritage in Social Welfare 1860–1930*. Metuchen, N.J.: Scarecrow Press, 1978.

Scott, J. A. (ed.). *Frances Ann Kemble's Journal of a Residence on a Georgia Plantation in 1838–1839*. New York: Alfred A. Knopf, 1961.

Shultz, David. *Coming Up Black*. Englewood Cliffs, N.J.: Prentice-Hall, 1969.

Silberman, Charles. *Crisis in Black and White*. New York: Random House, 1964.

Simmons, William J. *Men of Mark*. 1887. Reprint. New York: Arno Press, 1968.

Solomon, Barbara Bryant. *Black Empowerment: Social Work in Oppressed Communities*. New York: Columbia University Press, 1976.

Stack, Carol. *All Our Kin*. New York: Harper & Row, 1974.

Sweet, Leonard T. *Black Images of America: 1784–1870*. New York: W. W. Norton & Co., 1976.

Terborg-Penn, Rosalyn. "Black Male Perspectives on the Nineteenth Century Woman," in S. Harley and Rosalyn Terborg-Penn, eds., *The Afro-American Woman: Struggles and Images*. Port Washington, N.Y.: Kennikat Press, 1978, pp. 28–43.

Walker, David. *An Appeal to the Colored People of the World*. 1829. Reprint. New York: Arno Press, 1969.

Washington, Joseph R. *Black Religion*. Boston: Beacon Press, 1972.

Young, James O. *Black Writers of the Thirties*. Baton Rouge: Louisiana State University Press, 1973.

INDEX

Brown Fellowship Society, 40
Brown, John, 54
Burroughs, Nannie Helen, 56

C

Cayton, Horace, 46
Cheek, William F., 46
Christ, Jesus, 20, 27, 38, 39
Christianity, 17, 27–28, 68–69, 84
Civil War, 49–50, 93–94
    and black male heroism,
      49–50
    impact on slave and free black
      families, 49–51
    Union troops and black
      women, 49–50
Cleveland National Convention
    of 1848, 43
Cobbs, Price M., 64, 75
Collins, Alice H., 83, 90
Colonization societies, 34
Cones, James H., 52, 60
Conrad, Earl, 46
Cooper, Anna J., 56
Cooper, Frederick, 41, 46
Council on Social Work Education,
    87
Cox, Oliver C., 7, 9, 57, 60

D

Davis, Angela, 19, 30
Delaney, Martin, 35, 42, 45, 46,
    47
Desegregation, 62–63, 80–81, 82
Diggs, William, 77, 89
Douglass, Frederick, 35, 37, 38,
    39, 46, 50–51, 60
Drake, St. Clair, 46
Du Bois, W. E. B., 2, 7, 9,
    19–20, 53–54, 59, 60, 61, 62,
    63, 75

E

Ellison, Ralph, 3, 9
English Poor Law, 7

F

Father Divine, 79
Ferguson, Catherine, 57
Fictive kinship, 5, 35, 66, 92–93
    among free blacks, 35
    defined, 4
    in slavery, 22–23
    in traditional Africa, 15
Fleetwood, Sarah, 55
Fleming, Mary C., 53
Forten, Charlotte, 44
Forten, James, Jr., 42
Fraternal orders, 2, 37, 39–41,
    82, 93
    during Reconstruction, 54
    role of black women in, 45
    in urban America, 66
Frazier, E. Franklin, 1–2, 9, 15, 21,
    29, 30, 60, 64, 71, 75, 76, 80, 90
Free African Society, 40
Free blacks
    compared to slaves, 33
    identification with slaves, 34, 35
    helping tradition among,
      34–35, 37–38, 77–78, 92–94
Freedmen's Bureau, 7, 52, 78
Freud, Sigmund, 8, 84
Fugitive Slave Law, 43, 93

G

Garvey, Marcus, 61
Genovese, Eugene, 19, 23, 24,
    30, 31
Glazer, Nathan, 1, 9
God, 3, 27–28, 50, 51, 52, 79, 92
    and slave religion, 27–28

Sweet, Leonard T., 37, 46

T

"Talented tenth," 61
Temperance, 43, 56
Tennessee Valley Authority,
 79–80
Terborg-Penn, Rosalyn, 47
Terrell, Mary Church, 56
Theory, 2, 3, 5, 80
 defined, 3
Tourgee, Albion W., 53
Tradition
 defined, 4
 social scientists' view of, in
  black community, 1–4, 91
 Truth, Sojourner, 20, 35, 39,
  44, 45
 Tubman, Harriet, 35, 39

U

Uncle Tom, 25, 35, 58
Underground Railroad, 7, 35,
 43

Universal Negro Improvement
 Association, 61
Urbanization
 and decline of helping
  tradition, 63–65, 69, 79–80,
  82, 94, 95

V

Veterans Hospital in Tuskegee,
 Alabama, 63

W

Walker, David, 35, 42, 46
Washington, Booker T., 78
Washington, Joseph R., 51, 60
Watkins, Frances Ellen, 35, 44
Wells, Ida B., 56
White, Walter, 81
Women's clubs, 2, 45, 55–57, 82,
 94
Woodson, Carter G., 7
World War I, 63
World War II, 80
Young, Donald, 81, 90